ENVY AND GRATITUDE

ENVY AND GRATITUDE

A STUDY OF
UNCONSCIOUS SOURCES

———

MELANIE KLEIN

TAVISTOCK PUBLICATIONS LIMITED

First published in 1957
by Tavistock Publications (1959) Limited
11 New Fetter Lane, London, E.C.4

Second impression 1962

Printed in Great Britain
by Charles Birchall & Sons Limited
Liverpool and London

CONTENTS

ACKNOWLEDGMENTS page vii

PREFACE ix

ONE 1

TWO 10

THREE 22

FOUR 28

FIVE 43

SIX 61

SEVEN 70

CONCLUSION 84

BIBLIOGRAPHY 92

INDEX 95

ACKNOWLEDGMENTS

I wish to express my deep gratitude to my friend Lola Brook who has worked with me throughout the preparation of this book, as with many of my writings. She has a rare understanding of my work and has helped me with formulations and criticisms of the content at every stage. My thanks are also due to Dr Elliott Jaques who has made a number of valuable suggestions while the book was still in manuscript and has helped me by working on the proofs. I am indebted to Miss Judith Fay who took great trouble over making the index.

PREFACE

I HAVE for many years been interested in the earliest sources of two attitudes that have always been familiar —envy and gratitude. I arrived at the conclusion that envy is a most potent factor in undermining feelings of love and gratitude at their root, since it affects the earliest relation of all, that to the mother. The fundamental importance of this relation for the individual's whole emotional life has been substantiated in a number of psycho-analytic writings, and I think that by exploring further a particular factor that can be very disturbing at this early stage, I have added something of significance to my findings concerning infantile development and personality formation.

I consider that envy is an oral-sadistic and anal-sadistic expression of destructive impulses, operative from the beginning of life, and that it has a constitutional basis. These conclusions have certain important elements in common with Karl Abraham's work, and yet imply some differences from it. Abraham found that envy is an oral trait, but —and this is where my views differ from his—he assumed that envy and hostility operate at a later period, which, according to his hypothesis, constituted a second, the oral-sadistic, stage. Abraham did not speak of gratitude, but he described generosity as an oral feature. He considered the anal elements as an important component in envy, and stressed their derivation from oral-sadistic impulses.

A further fundamental point of agreement is Abraham's assumption of a constitutional element in the strength of oral impulses, which he linked with the aetiology of manic-depressive illness.

Above all, both Abraham's work and my own brought out more fully and more deeply the significance of destructive impulses. In his 'Short History of the Development of the Libido, Viewed in the Light of Mental Disorders', written in 1924 (*Selected Papers*), Abraham did not mention Freud's hypothesis of the life and death instincts, although *Beyond the Pleasure Principle* had been published four years previously. However, in his book Abraham explored the roots of destructive impulses and applied this understanding to the aetiology of mental disturbances more specifically than had ever been done before. It appears to me that although he had not made use of Freud's concept of the life and death instincts, his clinical work, particularly the analysis of the first manic-depressive patients to be analysed, was based on insight which was taking him in that direction. I would assume that Abraham's early death prevented his realizing the full implications of his own findings and their essential connection with Freud's discovery of the two instincts.

As I am about to publish this book, three decades after Abraham's death, it is a source of great satisfaction to me that my work has contributed to the growing recognition of the full significance of Abraham's discoveries.

CHAPTER ONE

I N THIS book I intend to make some further suggestions concerning the earliest emotional life of the infant and also to draw some conclusions about adulthood and mental health. It is inherent in Freud's discoveries that the exploration of the patient's past, of his childhood, and of his unconscious is a precondition for understanding his adult personality. Freud discovered the Oedipus complex in the adult and reconstructed from such material not only details of the Oedipus complex but also its timing. Abraham's findings have added considerably to this approach, which has become characteristic of the psycho-analytic method. We should also remember that, according to Freud, the conscious part of the mind develops out of the unconscious. Therefore, in tracing to early infancy material that I found first of all in the analysis of young children, and subsequently in that of adults, I followed a procedure now familiar in psycho-analysis. Observations of young children soon confirmed Freud's findings. I believe that some of the conclusions that I reached regarding a much earlier stage, the first years of life, can also be confirmed up to a point by observation. The right—indeed the necessity—to reconstruct from the material presented to us by our patients details and data about earlier stages is most convincingly described by Freud in the following passage:

'What we are in search of is a picture of the patient's forgotten years that shall be alike trustworthy and in all essential respects complete . . . His (the psycho-analyst's) work of construction, or, if it is preferred, of reconstruction, resembles to a great extent an archaeologist's excavation of some dwelling-place that has been destroyed and buried or of some ancient edifice. The two processes are in fact identical, except that the analyst works under better conditions and has more material at his command to assist him, since what he is dealing with is not something destroyed but something that is still alive—and perhaps for another reason as well. But just as the archaeologist builds up the walls of the building from the foundations that have remained standing, determines the number and position of the columns from depressions in the floor and reconstructs the mural decorations and paintings from the remains found in the debris, so does the analyst proceed when he draws his inferences from the fragments of memories, from the associations and from the behaviour of the subject of the analysis. Both of them have an undisputed right to reconstruct by means of supplementing and combining the surviving remains. Both of them, moreover, are subject to many of the same difficulties and sources of error . . . The analyst, as we have said, works under more favourable conditions than the archaeologist since he has at his disposal material which can have no counterpart in excavations, such as the repetition of reactions dating from infancy and all that emerges in connection with these repetitions through the transference. All of these essentials are preserved, even things that seem completely forgotten are present somehow and somewhere, and have merely been buried and made inaccessible to the subject. Indeed, it may, as we know, be doubted whether any psychical structure can really be the victim of total destruction. It depends only upon analytic technique whether we shall succeed in bringing what is concealed completely to light.'[1]

Experience has taught me that the complexity of the fully grown personality can only be understood if we gain insight into the mind of the baby and follow up its development into later life. That is to say, analysis makes its way from adulthood to infancy, and through intermediate stages back to adulthood, in a recurrent to-and-fro movement according to the prevalent transference situation.

Throughout my work I have attributed fundamental importance to the infant's first object relation—the relation to the mother's breast and to the mother—and have drawn the conclusion that if this primal object, which is introjected, takes root in the ego with relative security, the basis for a satisfactory development is laid. Innate factors contribute to this bond. Under the dominance of oral impulses, the breast is instinctively felt to be the source of nourishment and therefore, in a deeper sense, of life itself. This mental and physical closeness to the gratifying breast in some measure restores, if things go well, the lost prenatal unity with the mother and the feeling of security that goes with it. This largely depends on the infant's capacity to cathect sufficiently the breast or its symbolic representative, the bottle; in this way the mother is turned into a loved object. It may well be that his having formed part of the mother in the pre-natal state contributes to the infant's innate feeling that there exists outside him something that will give him all he needs and desires. The good breast is taken in and becomes part of the ego, and the infant who was first inside the mother now has the mother inside himself.

While the pre-natal state no doubt implies a feeling of unity and security, how far this state is undisturbed must depend on the psychological and physical condition of the

[1] 'Constructions in Analysis' (1937), *Collected Papers*, Vol. V.

mother, and possibly even on certain still unexplored factors in the unborn infant. We might, therefore, consider the universal longing for the pre-natal state also partly as an expression of the urge for idealization. If we investigate this longing in the light of idealization, we find that one of its sources is the strong persecutory anxiety stirred up by birth. We might speculate that this first form of anxiety possibly extends to the unborn infant's unpleasant experiences which, together with the feeling of security in the womb, foreshadow the double relation to the mother: the good and the bad breast.

External circumstances play a vital part in the initial relation to the breast. If birth has been difficult, and in particular if it results in complications such as lack of oxygen, a disturbance in the adaptation to the external world occurs and the relation to the breast starts at a great disadvantage. In such cases the baby's ability to experience new sources of gratification is impaired and in consequence he cannot sufficiently internalize a really good primal object. Furthermore, whether or not the child is adequately fed and mothered, whether the mother fully enjoys the care of the child or is anxious and has psychological difficulties over feeding—all these factors influence the infant's capacity to accept the milk with enjoyment and to internalize the good breast.

An element of frustration by the breast is bound to enter into the infant's earliest relation to it, because even a happy feeding situation cannot altogether replace the pre-natal unity with the mother. Also, the infant's longing for an inexhaustible and ever-present breast stems by no means only from a craving for food and from libidinal desires. For the urge even in the earliest stages to get constant evidence of the mother's love is fundamentally rooted in anxiety. The struggle between life and death instincts and the ensuing threat of annihilation of the self and of the object by destructive impulses are fundamental factors in the infant's initial relation to his mother. For his desires imply that the breast, and soon the mother, should do away with these destructive impulses and the pain of persecutory anxiety.

Together with happy experiences, unavoidable grievances reinforce the innate conflict between love and hate, in fact, basically between life and death instincts, and result in the feeling that a good and a bad breast exist. As a consequence, early emotional life is characterized by a sense of losing and regaining the good object. In speaking of an innate conflict between love and hate, I am implying that the capacity both for love and for destructive impulses is, to some extent, constitutional, though varying individually in strength and interacting from the beginning with external conditions.

I have repeatedly put forward the hypothesis that the primal good object, the mother's breast, forms the core of the ego and vitally contributes to its growth, and have often described how the infant feels that he concretely internalizes the breast and the milk it gives. Also there is in his mind already some indefinite connection between the breast and other parts and aspects of the mother.

I would not assume that the breast is to him merely a physical object. The whole of his instinctual desires and his unconscious phantasies imbue the breast with qualities going far beyond the actual nourishment it affords.[1]

We find in the analysis of our patients that the breast in

[1] All this is felt by the infant in much more primitive ways than language can express. When these pre-verbal emotions and phantasies are revived in the transference situation, they appear as 'memories in feelings', as I would call them, and are reconstructed and put into words with the help of the analyst. In the same way, words have to be used when we are reconstructing and describing other phenomena belonging to the early stages of development. In fact we cannot translate the language of the unconscious into consciousness without lending it words from our conscious realm.

its good aspect is the prototype of maternal goodness, in-exhaustible patience and generosity, as well as of creative-ness. It is these phantasies and instinctual needs that so en-rich the primal object that it remains the foundation for hope, trust, and belief in goodness.

This book deals with a particular aspect of earliest object relations and internalization processes that is rooted in orality. I am referring to the effects of envy on the develop-ment of the capacity for gratitude and happiness. Envy con-tributes to the infant's difficulties in building up his good object, for he feels that the gratification of which he was deprived has been kept for itself by the breast that frus-trated him.[1]

A distinction should be drawn between envy, jealousy, and greed. Envy is the angry feeling that another person possesses and enjoys something desirable—the envious impulse being to take it away or to spoil it. Moreover, envy implies the subject's relation to one person only and goes back to the earliest exclusive relation with the mother. Jealousy is based on envy, but involves a relation to at least two people; it is mainly concerned with love that the sub-

---

[1] In a number of my writings, *The Psycho-Analysis of Children*, 'The Early Stages of the Oedipus Complex' in *Contributions to Psycho-Analysis*, and *Developments in Psycho-Analysis*, I have referred to envy, arising from oral-, urethral-, and anal-sadistic sources, during the earliest stages of the Oedipus complex and connected it with the desire to spoil the mother's possessions, in particular the father's penis which in the infant's phantasy she contains. Already in my paper 'An Obsessional Neurosis in a Six-Year-Old Girl', which was read in 1924 but not published until it appeared in the *Psycho-Analysis of Children*, envy bound up with oral-, urethral-, and anal-sadistic attacks on her mother's body played a prominent role. But I had not related this envy specifically to the desire to take away and to spoil the mother's breasts, although I had come very near to these conclusions. In my paper 'On Identification' (*New Directions in Psycho-Analysis*), I discussed envy as a very important factor in projective identification. As far back as my *Psycho-Analy-sis of Children* I suggested that not only oral-sadistic but also urethral-sadistic and anal-sadistic trends are operative in very young infants.

ject feels is his due and has been taken away, or is in danger of being taken away, from him by his rival. In the everyday conception of jealousy, a man or a woman feels deprived of the loved person by somebody else.

Greed is an impetuous and insatiable craving, exceeding what the subject needs and what the object is able and willing to give. At the unconscious level, greed aims primarily at completely scooping out, sucking dry, and devouring the breast: that is to say, its aim is destructive introjection; whereas envy not only seeks to rob in this way, but also to put badness, primarily bad excrements and bad parts of the self, into the mother, and first of all into her breast, in order to spoil and destroy her. In the deepest sense this means destroying her creativeness. This process, which derives from urethral- and anal-sadistic impulses, I have elsewhere defined[1] as a destructive aspect of projective identification starting from the beginning of life.[2] One essential difference between greed and envy, although no rigid dividing line can be drawn since they are so closely associated, would accordingly be that greed is mainly bound up with introjection and envy with projection.

According to the *Shorter Oxford Dictionary*, jealousy means that somebody else has taken, or is given, 'the good' which by right belongs to the individual. In this context I would interpret 'the good' basically as the good breast, the mother, a loved person, whom somebody else has taken away. According to Crabb's *English Synonyms*, ' . . . Jeal-

---

[1] 'Notes on Some Schizoid Mechanisms' (*Developments in Psycho-Analysis*).

[2] Dr Elliott Jaques has drawn my attention to the etymological root of *envy* in the Latin *invidia*, which comes from the verb *invideo*—to look askance at, to look maliciously or spitefully into, to cast an evil eye upon, to envy or grudge anything. An early use is given in the phrase from Cicero, the translation of which is: 'to produce misfortune by his evil eye'. This confirms the differentiation I made between envy and greed in laying emphasis on the projective character of envy.

B

ousy fears to lose what it has; envy is pained at seeing another have that which it wants for itself . . . The envious man sickens at the sight of enjoyment. He is easy only in the misery of others. All endeavours therefore to satisfy an envious man are fruitless.' Jealousy, according to Crabb, is 'a noble or an ignoble passion according to the object. In the former case it is emulation sharpened by fear. In the latter case it is greediness stimulated by fear. Envy is always a base passion, drawing the worst passions in its train.'

The general attitude to jealousy differs from that to envy. In fact, in some countries (particularly in France) murder prompted by jealousy carries a less severe sentence. The reason for this distinction is to be found in a universal feeling that the murder of a rival may imply love for the unfaithful person. This means, in the terms discussed above, that love for 'the good' exists and that the loved object is not damaged and spoilt as it would be by envy.

Shakespeare's Othello, in his jealousy, destroys the object he loves and this, in my view, is characteristic of what Crabb described as an 'ignoble passion of jealousy'— greed stimulated by fear. A significant reference to jealousy as an inherent quality of the mind occurs in the same play:

> But jealous souls will not be answer'd so;
> They are not ever jealous for the cause,
> But jealous for they are jealous; 'tis a monster
> Begot upon itself, born on itself.

It could be said that the very envious person is insatiable, he can never be satisfied because his envy stems from within and therefore always finds an object to focus on. This shows also the close connection between jealousy, greed, and envy.

Shakespeare does not always seem to differentiate between envy and jealousy; the following lines from Othello fully show the significance of envy in the sense I have defined it here:

> Oh beware my Lord of jealousy;
> It is the green-eyed monster which doth mock
> The meat it feeds on . . .

One is reminded of the saying 'to bite the hand which feeds one', which is almost synonymous with biting, destroying, and spoiling the breast.

CHAPTER TWO

I

MY WORK has taught me that the first object to be envied is the feeding breast,[1] for the infant feels that it possesses everything he desires and that it has an unlimited flow of milk and love which the breast keeps for its own gratification. This feeling adds to his sense of grievance and hate, and the result is a disturbed relation to the mother. If envy is excessive, this, in my view, indicates that paranoid and schizoid features are abnormally strong and that such an infant can be regarded as ill.

Throughout this section I am speaking of the primary envy of the mother's breast, and this should be differentiated from its later forms (inherent in the girl's desire to take her mother's place and in the boy's feminine position) in which envy is no longer focused on the breast but on the mother receiving the father's penis, having babies inside her, giving birth to them, and being able to feed them.

I have often described the sadistic attacks on the mother's breast as determined by destructive impulses. Here I wish to add that envy gives particular impetus to these attacks. This means that when I wrote about the greedy scooping

[1] Joan Riviere, in her paper 'Jealousy as a Mechanism of Defence' (1932), traced envy in women to the infantile desire to rob the mother of her breasts and to spoil them. According to her findings, jealousy is rooted in this primal envy. Her paper contains interesting material illustrating these views.

out of the breast and of the mother's body, and the destruction of her babies, as well as putting bad excrements into the mother,[1] this adumbrated what I later came to recognize as the envious spoiling of the object.

If we consider that deprivation increases greed and persecutory anxiety, and that there is in the infant's mind a phantasy of an inexhaustible breast which is his greatest desire, it becomes understandable how envy arises even if the baby is inadequately fed. The infant's feelings seem to be that when the breast deprives him, it becomes bad because it keeps the milk, love, and care associated with the good breast all to itself. He hates and envies what he feels to be the mean and grudging breast.

It is perhaps more understandable that the satisfactory breast is also envied. The very ease with which the milk comes—though the infant feels gratified by it—also gives rise to envy because this gift seems something so unattainable.

We find this primitive envy revived in the transference situation. For instance: the analyst has just given an interpretation which brought the patient relief and produced a change of mood from despair to hope and trust. With some patients, or with the same patient at other times, this helpful interpretation may soon become the object of destructive criticism. It is then no longer felt to be something good he has received and has experienced as an enrichment. His criticism may attach itself to minor points; the interpretation should have been given earlier; it was too long, and has disturbed the patient's associations; or it was too short, and this implies that he has not been sufficiently understood. The envious patient grudges the analyst the success of his work; and if he feels that the analyst and the help he is giving have become spoilt and devalued by his envious

[1] Cf. my *Psycho-Analysis of Children*, where these concepts play a part in a number of connections.

criticism, he cannot introject him sufficiently as a good object nor accept his interpretations with real conviction and assimilate them. Real conviction, as we often see in less envious patients, implies gratitude for a gift received. The envious patient may also feel, because of guilt about devaluing the help given, that he is unworthy to benefit by analysis.

Needless to say, our patients criticize us for a variety of reasons, sometimes with justification. But a patient's need to devalue the analytic work which he has experienced as helpful is the expression of envy. In the transference we discover the root of envy if we trace back the emotional situations we encounter in earlier stages down to the primary one. Destructive criticism is particularly evident in paranoid patients who indulge in the sadistic pleasure of disparaging the analyst's work, even though it has given them some relief. In these patients envious criticism is quite open; in others it may play an equally important role but remains unexpressed and even unconscious. In my experience, the slow progress we make in such cases is also connected with envy. We find that their doubts and uncertainties about the value of the analysis persist. What happens is that the patient has split off the envious and hostile part of his self and constantly presents to the analyst other aspects that he feels to be more acceptable. Yet the split-off parts essentially influence the course of the analysis, which ultimately can only be effective if it achieves integration and deals with the whole of the personality. Other patients try to avoid criticism by becoming confused. This confusion is not only a defence but also expresses the uncertainty as to whether the analyst is still a good figure, or whether he and the help he is giving have become bad because of the patient's hostile criticism. This uncertainty I would trace back to the feelings of confusion that are one of the consequences of the disturbed earliest relation to the mother's breast. The infant who, owing to the strength of paranoid and schizoid mechanisms and the impetus of envy, cannot divide and keep apart successfully love and hate, and therefore the good and bad object, is liable to feel confused between what is good and bad in other connections.

In these ways envy, and the defences against it, play an important part in the negative therapeutic reaction, in addition to the factors discovered by Freud and further developed by Joan Riviere.[1]

For envy, and the attitudes it gives rise to, interfere with the gradual building up of a good object in the transference situation. If at the earliest stage the good food and the primal good object could not be accepted and assimilated, this is repeated in the transference and the course of the analysis is impaired.

In the context of the analytic material, it is possible by working through former situations to reconstruct the patient's feelings as a baby towards the mother's breast. For instance, the infant may have a grievance that the milk comes too quickly or too slowly;[2] or that he was not given the breast when he most craved for it, and therefore, when it is offered, he does not want it any more. He turns away from it and sucks his fingers instead. When he accepts the breast, he may not drink enough, or the feed is disturbed. Some infants obviously have great difficulty in overcoming such grievances. With others these feelings, even though

[1] 'A Contribution to the Analysis of the Negative Therapeutic Reaction', 1936; also Freud, *The Ego and the Id*.

[2] The baby may in fact have received too little milk, did not receive it at the time it was most wanted, or did not get it in the right way, for instance the milk came too quickly or too slowly. The way the infant was held, whether comfortable or not, the mother's attitude towards feeding, her pleasure in it or anxiety about it, whether the bottle or breast was given— all these factors are in every case of great importance.

based on actual frustrations, are soon overcome; the breast is taken and the feed is fully enjoyed. We find in analysis that patients who, according to what they have been told, took their food satisfactorily and showed no obvious signs of the attitudes I have just described, had split off their grievance, envy, and hate, which nevertheless form part of their character development. These processes become quite clear in the transference situation. The original wish to please the mother, the longing to be loved, as well as the urgent need to be protected from the consequences of their own destructive impulses, can be found in the analysis to underlie the co-operation of those patients whose envy and hate are split off but form part of the negative therapeutic reaction.

II

I have often referred to the infant's desire for the inexhaustible, ever-present breast. But as has been suggested in the previous section it is not only food he desires; he also wants to be freed from destructive impulses and persecutory anxiety. This feeling that the mother is omnipotent and that it is up to her to prevent all pain and evils from internal and external sources is also found in the analysis of adults. In passing, I would say that the very favourable changes in feeding children which have come about in recent years, in contrast to the rather rigid way of feeding according to timetable, cannot altogether prevent the infant's difficulties, because the mother cannot eliminate his destructive impulses and persecutory anxiety. There is another point to be considered. A too anxious attitude on the part of the mother who, whenever the infant cries, at once presents him with food, is unhelpful to the infant. He feels the mother's anxiety and this increases his own. I have also met in adults the grievance that they had not been allowed to cry enough, and thereby missed the possibility of expressing anxiety and grief (and thus getting relief) so that neither aggressive impulses nor depressive anxieties could sufficiently find an outlet. It is of interest that Abraham mentions, among the factors which underlie manic-depressive illness, both excessive frustration and too great indulgence.[1] For frustration, if not excessive, is also a stimulus for adaptation to the external world and for the development of the sense of reality. In fact, a certain amount of frustration followed by gratification might give the infant the feeling that he has been able to cope with his anxiety. I have also found that the infant's unfulfilled desires—which are to some extent incapable of fulfilment—are an important contributory factor to his sublimations and creative activities. The absence of conflict in the infant, if such a hypothetical state could be imagined, would deprive him of enrichment of his personality and of an important factor in the strengthening of his ego. For conflict, and the need to overcome it, is a fundamental element in creativeness.

From the contention that envy spoils the primal good object, and gives added impetus to sadistic attacks on the breast, further conclusions arise. The breast attacked in this way has lost its value, it has become bad by being bitten up and poisoned by urine and faeces. Excessive envy increases the *intensity* of such attacks and their *duration*, and thus makes it more difficult for the infant to regain the lost good object; whereas sadistic attacks on the breast that are less determined by envy pass more quickly, and therefore do not, in the infant's mind, so strongly and lastingly destroy the goodness of the object: the breast that returns

[1] 'A Short History of the Development of the Libido' (1924).

and can be enjoyed is felt as an evidence that it is not injured and that it is still good.[1]

The fact that envy spoils the capacity for enjoyment explains to some extent why envy is so persistent.[2] For it is *enjoyment* and the *gratitude* to which it gives rise that mitigate destructive impulses, envy, and greed. To look at it from another angle: greed, envy, and persecutory anxiety, which are bound up with each other, inevitably increase each other. The feeling of the harm done by envy, the great anxiety that stems from this, and the resulting uncertainty about the goodness of the object, have the effect of increasing greed and destructive impulses. Whenever the object is felt to be good after all, it is all the more greedily desired and taken in. This applies to food as well. In analysis we find that when a patient is in great doubt about his object, and therefore also about the value of the analyst and the analysis, he may cling to any interpretations that relieve his anxiety, and is inclined to prolong the session because he wants to take in as much as possible of what at the time he feels to be good. (Some people are so afraid of their greed that they are particularly keen to leave on time.)

Doubts in the possession of the good object and the corresponding uncertainty about one's own good feelings also contribute to greedy and indiscriminate identifications; such people are easily influenced because they cannot trust their own judgment.

[1] Observations of babies show us something of these underlying unconscious attitudes. As I have said above, some infants who have been screaming with rage appear quite happy soon after they begin to feed. This means that they have temporarily lost but regained their good object. With others, the persisting grievance and anxiety—even though they are for the moment diminished by the feed—can be gathered by careful observers.

[2] It is clear that deprivation, unsatisfactory feeding, and unfavourable circumstances intensify envy because they disturb full gratification, and a vicious circle is created.

In contrast with the infant who, owing to his envy, has been unable to build up securely a good internal object, a child with a strong capacity for love and gratitude has a deep-rooted relation with a good object and can, without being fundamentally damaged, withstand temporary states of envy, hatred, and grievance, which arise even in children who are loved and well mothered. Thus, when these negative states are transient, the good object is regained time and time again. This is an essential factor in establishing it and in laying the foundations of stability and a strong ego. In the course of development, the relation to the mother's breast becomes the foundation for devotion to people, values, and causes, and thus some of the love which was originally experienced for the primal object is absorbed.

III

One major derivative of the capacity for love is the feeling of gratitude. Gratitude is essential in building up the relation to the good object and underlies also the appreciation of goodness in others and in oneself. Gratitude is rooted in the emotions and attitudes that arise in the earliest stage of infancy, when for the baby the mother is the one and only object. I have referred to this early bond[1] as the basis for all later relations with one loved person. While the exclusive relation to the mother varies individually in duration and intensity, I believe that, up to a point, it exists in most people. How far it remains undisturbed depends partly on external circumstances. But the internal factors underlying it—above all the capacity for love—appear to be innate. Destructive impulses, especially strong envy, may at an early stage disturb this particular bond with the

[1] *Developments in Psycho-Analysis*, Chapter VI.

mother. If envy of the feeding breast is strong, the full gratification is interfered with because, as I have already described, it is characteristic of envy that it implies robbing the object of what it possesses, and spoiling it.

The infant can only experience complete enjoyment if the capacity for love is sufficiently developed; and it is enjoyment that forms the basis for gratitude. Freud described the infant's bliss in being suckled as the prototype of sexual gratification.[1] In my view these experiences constitute not only the basis of sexual gratification but of all later happiness and make possible the feeling of unity with another person; such unity means being fully understood, which is essential for every happy love relation or friendship. At best, such an understanding needs no words to express it, which demonstates its derivation from the earliest closeness with the mother in the pre-verbal stage. The capacity to enjoy fully the first relation to the breast forms the foundation for experiencing pleasure from various sources.

If the undisturbed enjoyment in being fed is frequently experienced, the introjection of the good breast comes about with relative security. A full gratification at the breast means that the infant feels he has received from his loved object a unique gift which he wants to keep. This is the basis of gratitude. Gratitude is closely linked with the trust in good figures. This includes first of all the ability to accept and assimilate the loved primal object (not only as a source of food) without greed and envy interfering too much; for greedy internalization disturbs the relation to the object. The individual feels that he is controlling and exhausting, and therefore injuring it, whereas in a good relation to the internal and external object, the wish to preserve and spare it predominates. I have described in

[1] *Three Essays on the Theory of Sexuality.*

another connection[1] the process underlying the belief in the good breast as derived from the infant's capacity to invest the first external object with libido. In this way a good object is established,[2] which loves and protects the self and is loved and protected by the self. This is the basis for trust in one's own goodness.

The more often gratification at the breast is experienced and fully accepted, the more often enjoyment and gratitude, and accordingly the wish to return pleasure, are felt. This recurrent experience makes possible gratitude on the deepest level and plays an important role in the capacity to make reparation, and in all sublimations. Through processes of projection and introjection, through inner wealth given out and re-introjected, an enrichment and deepening of the ego comes about. In this way the possession of the helpful inner object is again and again re-established and gratitude can fully come into play.

Gratitude is closely bound up with generosity. Inner wealth derives from having assimilated the good object so that the individual becomes able to share its gifts with others. This makes it possible to introject a more friendly outer world, and a feeling of enrichment ensues. Even the fact that generosity is often insufficiently appreciated does not necessarily undermine the ability to give. By contrast, with people in whom this feeling of inner wealth and strength is not sufficiently established, bouts of generosity are often followed by an exaggerated need for appreciation and gratitude, and consequently by persecutory anxieties of having been impoverished and robbed.

Strong envy of the feeding breast interferes with the

[1] *Developments in Psycho-Analysis*, Ch. VII.

[2] Cf. also Donald Winnicott's concept of the 'illusory breast' and his view that at the beginning the objects are created by the self ('Psychoses and Child Care', 1953).

capacity for complete enjoyment, and thus undermines the development of gratitude. There are very pertinent psychological reasons why envy ranks among the seven 'deadly sins'. I would even suggest that it is unconsciously felt to be the greatest sin of all, because it spoils and harms the good object which is the source of life. This view is consistent with the view described by Chaucer in *The Parsons Tale*: 'It is certain that envy is the worst sin that is; for all other sins are sins only against one virtue, whereas envy is against all virtue and against all goodness.' The feeling of having injured and destroyed the primal object impairs the individual's trust in the sincerity of his later relations and makes him doubt his capacity for love and goodness.

We frequently encounter expressions of gratitude which turn out to be prompted mainly by feelings of guilt and much less by the capacity for love. I think the distinction between such guilty feelings and gratitude on the deepest level is important. This does not mean that some element of guilt does not enter into the most genuine feelings of gratitude.

My observations have shown me that significant changes in character, which at close quarters reveal themselves as character deterioration, are much more likely to happen in persons who have not established their first object securely and are not capable of maintaining gratitude towards it. When in those people persecutory anxiety increases for internal or external reasons, they lose completely their primal good object, or rather its substitutes, be it persons or values. The processes that underlie this change are a regressive return to early splitting mechanisms and disintegration. Since this is a matter of degree, such a disintegration, though ultimately it strongly affects character, does not necessarily lead to manifest illness. The craving for power and prestige, or the need to pacify persecutors at any cost, are among the aspects of the character changes I have in mind.

I have seen in some cases that when envy of a person arises, the feeling of envy from its earliest sources is activated. Since these primary feelings are of an omnipotent nature, this reflects on the current feeling of envy experienced towards a substitute figure and contributes, therefore, both to the emotions stirred by envy as well as to despondency and guilt. It seems likely that this activation of the earliest envy by a common experience is common to everyone, but both the degree and the intensity of the feeling, as well as the feeling of omnipotent destruction, vary with the individual. This factor may prove to be of great importance in the analysis of envy for only if it can reach down to its deeper sources is the analysis likely to take full effect.

No doubt, in every individual, frustration and unhappy circumstances rouse some envy and hate throughout life, but the strength of these emotions and the way in which the individual copes with them varies considerably. This is one of the many reasons why the capacity for enjoyment, bound up with a feeling of gratitude for goodness received, differs vastly in people.

CHAPTER THREE

I

To clarify my argument, some reference to my views on the early ego seems necessary. I believe that it exists from the beginning of post-natal life, though in a rudimentary form and largely lacking coherence. Already at the earliest stage it performs a number of important functions. It might well be that this early ego approximates to the unconscious part of the ego postulated by Freud. Though he did not assume that an ego exists from the beginning, he attributed to the organism a function which, as I see it, can only be performed by the ego. The threat of annihiliation by the death instinct within is, in my view—which differs from Freud's on this point[1]—the primordial anxiety, and it is the ego which, in the service of the life instinct—possibly even called into operation by the life instinct—deflects to some extent that threat outwards. This fundamental defence against the death instinct Freud attributed to the organism, whereas I regard this process as the prime activity of the ego.

There are other primal activities of the ego which, in my view, derive from the imperative need to deal with the struggle between life and death instincts. One of these func-

[1] Freud stated that 'the unconscious seems to contain nothing that would lend substance to the concept of the annihilation of life'. *Inhibitions, Symptoms and Anxiety*, p. 93.

tions is gradual integration which stems from the life instinct and expresses itself in the capacity for love. The opposite tendency of the ego to split itself and its objects occurs in part because the ego largely lacks cohesion at birth, and in part because it constitutes a defence against the primordial anxiety, and is therefore a means of preserving the ego. I have, for many years, attributed great importance to one particular process of splitting: the division of the breast into a good and a bad object. I took this to be an expression of the innate conflict between love and hate and of the ensuing anxieties. However, co-existing with this division, there appear to be various processes of splitting, and it is only in recent years that some of them have been more clearly understood. For instance, I found that concurrently with the greedy and devouring internalization of the object—first of all the breast—the ego in varying degrees fragments itself and its objects, and in this way achieves a dispersal of the destructive impulses and of internal persecutory anxieties. This process, varying in strength and determining the greater or lesser normality of the individual, is one of the defences during the paranoid-schizoid position, which I believe normally extends over the first three or four months of life.[1] I am not suggesting that during that period the infant is not capable of fully enjoying his feeds, the relation to his mother, and frequent states of physical comfort or well-being. But whenever anxiety arises, it is mainly of a paranoid nature and the defences against it, as well as the mechanisms used, are predominantly schizoid. The same applies, *mutatis mutandis*, to the infant's emotional life during the period characterized by the depressive position.

To return to the splitting process, which I take to be a

[1] Cf. my 'Notes on Some Schizoid Mechanisms'; also Herbert Rosenfeld 'Analysis of a Schizophrenic State with Depersonalization' (1947).

pre-condition for the young infant's relative stability; during the first few months he predominantly keeps the good object apart from the bad one and thus, in a fundamental way, preserves it—which also means that the security of the ego is enhanced. At the same time, this primal division only succeeds if there is an adequate capacity for love and a relatively strong ego. My hypothesis is, therefore, that the capacity for love gives impetus both to integrating tendencies and to a successful primal splitting between the loved and hated object. This sounds paradoxical. But since, as I said, integration is based on a strongly rooted good object that forms the core of the ego, a certain amount of splitting is essential for integration; for it preserves the good object and later on enables the ego to synthesize the two aspects of it. Excessive envy, an expression of destructive impulses, interferes with the primal split between the good and bad breast, and the building up of a good object cannot sufficiently be achieved. Thus the basis is not laid for a fully developed and integrated adult personality; for the later differentiation between good and bad is disturbed in various connections. In so far as this disturbance of development is due to excessive envy, it derives from the prevalence, in the earliest stages, of paranoid and schizoid mechanisms which, according to my hypothesis, form the basis of schizophrenia.

II

In the exploration of early splitting processes, it is essential to differentiate between a good object and an idealized one, though this distinction cannot be drawn sharply. A very deep split between the two aspects of the object indicates that it is not the good and bad object that are being kept apart but an idealized and an extremely bad one. So deep and sharp a division reveals that destructive impulses, envy, and persecutory anxiety are very strong and that idealization serves mainly as a defence against these emotions.

If the good object is deeply rooted, the split is fundamentally of a different nature and allows the all-important processes of ego integration and object synthesis to operate. Thus a mitigation of hatred by love can come about in some measure and the depressive position can be worked through. As a result, the identification with a good and whole object is the more securely established; and this also lends strength to the ego and enables it to preserve its identity as well as a feeling of possessing goodness of its own. It becomes less liable to identify indiscriminately with a variety of objects, a process that is characteristic of a weak ego. Furthermore, full identification with a good object goes with a feeling of the self possessing goodness of its own. When things go wrong, excessive projective identification, by which split-off parts of the self are projected into the object, leads to a strong confusion between the self and the object, which also comes to stand for the self.[1] Bound up with this is a weakening of the ego and a grave disturbance in object relations.

Infants whose capacity for love is strong feel less need for idealization than those in whom destructive impulses and persecutory anxiety are paramount. Excessive idealization denotes that persecution is the main driving force. As I discovered many years ago in my work with young children, idealization is a corollary of persecutory anxiety—a defence against it—and the ideal breast is the counterpart of the devouring breast.

The idealized object is much less integrated in the ego

---

[1] I have dealt with the importance of this process in earlier writings and only wish to stress here that it seems to me a fundamental mechanism in the paranoid-schizoid position.

than the good object, since it stems predominantly from persecutory anxiety and much less from the capacity for love. I also found that idealization derives from the innate feeling that an extremely good breast exists, a feeling which leads to the longing for a good object and for the capacity to love it.[1] This appears to be a condition for life itself, that is to say, an expression of the life instinct. Since the need for a good object is universal, the distinction between an idealized and a good object cannot be considered as absolute.

Some people deal with their incapacity (derived from excessive envy) to possess a good object by idealizing it. This first idealization is precarious, for the envy experienced towards the good object is bound to extend to its idealized aspect. The same is true of idealizations of further objects and the identification with them, which is often unstable and indiscriminate. Greed is an important factor in these indiscriminate identifications, for the need to get the best from everywhere interferes with the capacity for selection and discrimination. This incapacity is also bound up with the confusion between good and bad that arises in the relation to the primal object.

While people who have been able to establish the primal good object with relative security are capable of retaining their love for it in spite of its shortcomings, with others idealization is a characteristic of their love relations and friendships. This tends to break down and then one loved object may frequently have to be exchanged for another; for none can come fully up to expectations. The former idealized person is often felt as a persecutor (which shows the origin of

[1] I have already referred to the inherent need to idealize the pre-natal situation. Another frequent field for idealization is the baby-mother relation. It is particularly those people who were not able to experience sufficient happiness in this relation who idealize it in retrospect.

idealization as a counterpart to persecution), and into him is projected the subject's envious and critical attitude. It is of great importance that similar processes operate in the internal world which in this way comes to contain particularly dangerous objects. All this leads to instability in relationships. This is another aspect of the weakness of the ego, to which I referred earlier in connection with indiscriminate identifications.

Doubts connected with the good object easily arise even in a secure child-mother relation; this is not only due to the fact that the infant is very dependent on the mother, but also to the recurrent anxiety that his greed and his destructive impulses will get the better of him—an anxiety which is an important factor in depressive states. However, at any stage of life, under the stress of anxiety, the belief and trust in good objects can be shaken; but it is the *intensity* and *duration* of such states of doubt, despondency, and persecution that determine whether the ego is capable of reintegrating itself and of reinstating its good objects securely.[1] Hope and trust in the existence of goodness, as can be observed in everyday life, helps people through great adversity, and effectively counteracts persecution.

[1] In this connection I refer to my paper on 'Mourning and its relation to Manic-Depressive States' (*Contributions to Psycho-Analysis*) in which I defined the normal working-through of mourning as a process during which the early good objects are reinstated. I suggested that this working-through first takes place when the infant successfully deals with the depressive position.

CHAPTER FOUR

I

IT APPEARS that one of the consequences of excessive envy is an early onset of guilt. If premature guilt is experienced by an ego not yet capable of bearing it, guilt is felt as persecution and the object that rouses guilt is turned into a persecutor. The infant then cannot work—through either depressive or persecutory anxiety because they become confused with each other. A few months later, when the depressive position arises, the more integrated and stronger ego has a greater capacity to bear the pain of guilt and to develop corresponding defences, mainly the tendency to make reparation.

The fact that in the earliest stage (i.e. during the paranoid-schizoid position) premature guilt increases persecution and disintegration, brings the consequence that the working-through of the depressive position also fails.[1]

---

[1] Whereas I have not altered my views on the depressive position setting in about the second quarter of the first year and coming to a climax at about six months, I have found that some infants seem to experience guilt transiently in the first few months of life (Cf. *Developments in Psycho-Analysis*, Ch. VIII). This does not imply that the depressive position has already arisen. I have elsewhere described the variety of processes and defences that characterize the depressive position, such as the relation to the whole object; stronger recognition of internal and external reality; defences against depression, in particular the urge for reparation, and the widening of object relations lead-

This failure can be observed in both child and adult patients: as soon as guilt is felt, the analyst becomes persecutory and is accused on many grounds. In such cases we find that as infants they could not experience guilt without its simultaneously leading to persecutory anxiety with its corresponding defences. These defences appear later as projection on to the analyst and omnipotent denial.

It is my hypothesis that one of the deepest sources of guilt is always linked with the envy of the feeding breast, and with the feeling of having spoilt its goodness by envious attacks. If the primal object has been established with relative stability in early infancy, the guilt aroused by such feelings can be coped with more successfully because then envy is more transient and less liable to endanger the relation to the good object.

Excessive envy interferes with adequate oral gratification and so acts as a stimulus towards the intensification of genital desires and trends. This implies that the infant turns too early towards genital gratification, with the consequence that the oral relation becomes genitalized and the genital trends become too much coloured by oral grievances and anxieties. I have often contended that genital sensations and desires are possibly operative from birth onwards; for instance, it is well known that infant boys have erections at a very early stage. But in speaking of these sensations arising prematurely I mean that genital trends interfere with oral ones at a stage when normally the oral desires are upper-

ing to the early stages of the Oedipus complex. In speaking about guilt transiently experienced in the first stage of life, I came closer to the view I held at the time when I wrote the *Psycho-Analysis of Children*, where I described guilt and persecution experienced by very young infants. When later on I defined the depressive position, I divided more clearly, and perhaps too schematically, guilt, depression, and the corresponding defences on the one hand, and the paranoid stage (which I later called the paranoid-schizoid position) on the other.

most.[1] Here again we have to consider the effects of early confusion, which expresses itself in a blurring of the oral, anal, and genital impulses and phantasies. An overlapping between these various sources both of libido and of aggressiveness is normal. But when the overlapping amounts to an incapacity to experience sufficiently the predominance of either of these trends at their proper stage of development, then both later sexual life and sublimations are adversely affected. Genitality based on a flight from orality is insecure because into it are carried over the suspicions and disappointments attaching to the impaired oral enjoyment. The interference with oral primacy by genital trends undermines the gratification in the genital sphere and often is the cause of obsessional masturbation and of promiscuity. For the lack of the primary enjoyment introduces into the genital desires compulsive elements and, as I have seen with some patients, may therefore lead to sexual sensations entering into all activities, thought processes, and interests. With some infants, the flight into genitality is also a defence against hating and injuring the first object towards which ambivalent feelings operate. I have found that the premature onset of genitality may be bound up with the early occurrence of guilt and is characteristic of paranoid and schizoid cases.[2]

When the infant reaches the depressive position, and becomes more able to face his psychic reality, he also feels that the object's badness is largely due to his own aggres-

---

[1] I have reason to believe that this premature genitalization is often a feature in strong schizophrenic traits or in full-blown schizophrenia. Cf. W. Bion in 'Notes on the Theory of Schizophrenia' (1954) and 'Differentiation of the Psychotic from the Non-Psychotic Personalities' (1955).

[2] Cf. 'The Importance of Symbol-Formation in the Development of the Ego' (1930) and 'A Contribution to the Psychogenesis of Manic-Depressive States' (1935), both in Contributions to Psycho-Analysis; also The Psycho-Analysis of Children.

siveness and the ensuing projection. This insight, as we can see in the transference situation, gives rise to great mental pain and guilt when the depressive position is at its height. But it also brings about feelings of relief and hope, which in turn make it less difficult to reunite the two aspects of the object and of the self and to work through the depressive position. This hope is based on the growing unconscious knowledge that the internal and external object is not as bad as it was felt to be in its split-off aspects. Through mitigation of hatred by love the object improves in the infant's mind. It is no longer so strongly felt to have been destroyed in the past and the danger of its being destroyed in the future is lessened; not being injured, it is also felt to be less vulnerable in the present and future. The internal object acquires a restraining and self-preservative attitude and its greater strength is an important aspect of its super-ego function.

In describing the overcoming of the depressive position, bound up with the greater trust in the good internal object, I do not intend to convey that such results cannot be temporarily undone. Strain of an internal or external nature is liable to stir up depression and distrust in the self as well as in the object. However, the capacity to emerge from such depressive states, and to regain one's feeling of inner security, is in my view the criterion of a well developed personality. By contrast, the frequent way of dealing with depression by hardening one's feelings and denying depression is a regression to the manic defences used during the infantile depressive position.

II

There is a direct link between the envy experienced towards the mother's breast and the development of jealousy.

Jealousy is based on the suspicion of and rivalry with the father, who is accused of having taken away the mother's breast and the mother. This rivalry marks the early stages of the direct and inverted Oedipus complex, which normally arises concurrently with the depressive position in the second quarter of the first year.[1]

The development of the Oedipus complex is strongly influenced by the vicissitudes of the first exclusive relation with the mother, and when this relation is disturbed too soon, the rivalry with the father enters prematurely. Phantasies of the penis inside the mother, or inside her breast, turn the father into a hostile intruder. This phantasy is particularly strong when the infant has not had the full enjoyment and happiness that the early relation to the mother can afford him and has not taken in the first good object with some security. Such failure partly depends on the strength of envy.

When in earlier writings I described the depressive position, I showed that at that stage the infant progressively integrates his feelings of love and hatred, synthesizes the good and bad aspects of the mother, and goes through states of mourning bound up with feelings of guilt. He also begins to understand more of the external world and realizes that he cannot keep his mother to himself as his exclusive possession. Whether or not the infant can find help against that grief in the relation to the second object, the father, or to other people in his surroundings, largely depends on the emotions which he experiences towards his lost unique object. If that relation was well founded, the fear of losing the mother is less strong and the capacity to share her is greater. Then he can also experience more

---

[1] I have pointed out elsewhere (e.g. in *Developments in Psycho-Analysis*, Ch. VI) the close connection between the phase in which the depressive position develops and the early stages of the Oedipus complex.

love towards his rivals. All this implies that he has been able to work through the depressive position satisfactorily, which in turn depends on envy towards the primal object not being excessive.

Jealousy is, as we know, inherent in the Oepidus situation and is accompanied by hate and death wishes. Normally, however, the gain of new objects who can be loved —the father and siblings—and other compensations which the developing ego derives from the external world, mitigate to some extent jealousy and grievance. If paranoid and schizoid mechanisms are strong, jealousy—and ultimately envy—remain unmitigated. The development of the Oedipus complex is essentially influenced by all these factors.

Among the features of the earliest stage of the Oedipus complex are the phantasies of the mother's breast and the mother containing the penis of the father, or the father containing the mother. This is the basis of the combined parent figure, and I have elaborated the importance of this phantasy in earlier writings.[1] The influence of the combined parent figure on the infant's ability to differentiate between the parents, and to establish good relations with each of them, is affected by the strength of envy and the intensity of his Oedipus jealousy. For the suspicion that the parents are always getting sexual gratification from one another reinforces the phantasy—derived from various sources—that they are always combined. If these anxieties are strongly operative, and therefore unduly prolonged, the consequence may be a lasting disturbance in the relation to both parents. In very ill individuals, the inability to

[1] *The Psycho-Analysis of Children* (particularly Ch. VIII) and *Developments in Psycho-Analysis* (Ch. VI). I have pointed out there that these phantasies form normally part of the early stages of the Oedipus complex but I would now add that the whole development of the Oedipus complex is strongly influenced by the intensity of envy which determines the strength of the combined parent figure.

disentangle the relation to the father from the one to the mother, because of their being inextricably interlinked in the patient's mind, plays an important role in severe states of confusion.

If envy is not excessive, jealousy in the Oedipus situation becomes a means of working it through. When jealousy is experienced, hostile feelings are directed not so much against the primal object but rather against the rivals—father or siblings—which brings in an element of distribution. At the same time, when these relations develop, they give rise to feelings of love, and become a new source of gratification. Furthermore, the change from oral desires to genital ones reduces the importance of the mother as a giver of oral enjoyment. (As we know, the object of envy is largely oral.) With the boy, a good deal of hate is deflected on to the father who is envied for the possession of the mother; this is the typical Oedipus jealousy. With the girl, the genital desires for the father enable her to find another loved object. Thus jealousy to some extent supersedes envy; the mother becomes the chief rival. The girl desires to take her mother's place and to possess and take care of the babies which the loved father gives to the mother. The identification with the mother in this role makes a wider range of sublimations possible. It is essential also to consider that the working-through of envy by means of jealousy is at the same time an important defence against envy. Jealousy is felt to be much more acceptable and gives rise much less to guilt than the primary envy which destroys the first good object.

In analysis we can often see the close connection between jealousy and envy. For instance, a patient felt very jealous of a man with whom he thought that I was in close personal contact. The next step was a feeling that in any case I was probably in private life uninteresting and boring, and suddenly the whole of the analysis appeared to him as boring. The interpretation—in this case by the patient himself—that this was a defence led to the recognition of a devaluation of the analyst as a result of an upsurge of envy.

Ambition is another factor highly instrumental in stirring up envy. This frequently relates first to the rivalry and competition in the Oedipus situation; but if excessive, it clearly shows its root in the envy of the primal object. Failure to fulfil one's ambition is often aroused by the conflict between the urge to make reparation to the object injured by destructive envy and a renewed reappearance of envy.

Freud's discovery of penis-envy in women and its link with aggressive impulses was a basic contribution to the understanding of envy. When penis-envy and castration wishes are strong, the envied object, the penis, is to be destroyed and the man who owns it is to be deprived of it. In his 'Analysis Terminable and Interminable'[1] Freud emphasized the difficulty arising in the analysis of women patients by the very fact that they can never acquire the penis that they desire. He stated that women patients feel 'an inner conviction that the analysis will avail them nothing and that they will be none the better for it; we can only agree with them when we discover that their strongest motive in coming for analysis was the hope that they might somehow still obtain a male organ, the lack of which is so painful to them'.

A number of factors contribute to penis-envy which I have discussed in other connections.[2] In this context I wish

[1] *Collected Papers*, Vol. V.

[2] *Contributions to Psycho-Analysis*, pp. 389–90: 'Penis envy and the castration complex play an essential part in the girl's development. But they are very much reinforced by frustration of her positive Oedipus desires. Though the little girl at one stage assumes that her mother possesses a penis as a male

to consider the woman's penis-envy mainly in so far as it is of oral origin. As we know, under the dominance of oral desires, the penis is strongly equated with the breast (Abraham) and in my experience the woman's penis-envy can be traced back to envy of the mother's breast. I have found that if the penis-envy of women is analysed on these lines, we can see that its root lies in the earliest relation to the mother, in the fundamental envy of the mother's breast, and in the destructive feelings allied with it.

Freud has shown how vital is the attitude of the girl to her mother in her subsequent relations to men. When envy of the mother's breast has been strongly transferred to the father's penis, the outcome may be a reinforcing of her homosexual attitude. Another outcome is a sudden and abrupt turning to the penis away from the breast, because of the excessive anxieties and conflicts to which the oral relation gives rise. This is essentially a flight mechanism and therefore does not lead to stable relations with the second object. If the main motive for this flight is envy and hatred experienced towards the mother, these emotions are soon transferred to the father, and therefore a lasting and loving attitude to him cannot be established. At the same time, the envious relation to the mother expresses itself in an excessive Oedipus rivalry. This rivalry is much less due to love of the father than to envy of the

attribute, this concept does not play nearly as important a part in her development as Freud suggests. The unconscious theory that her mother contains the admired and desired penis of the father underlies, in my experience, many of the phenomena which Freud described as the relation of the girl to the phallic mother. The girl's oral desires for her father's penis mingle with her first genital desires to receive that penis. These genital desires imply the wish to receive the children from her father, which is also borne out by the equation ''penis-child''. The feminine desire to internalize the penis and to receive a child from her father invariably precedes the wish to possess a penis of her own.'

mother's possession of the father and his penis. The envy experienced towards the breast is then fully carried over into the Oedipus situation. The father (or his penis) has become an appendage to the mother and it is on these grounds that the girl wants to rob her mother of him. Therefore in later life, every success in her relation to men becomes a victory over another woman. This applies even where there is no obvious rival, because the rivalry is then directed against the man's mother, as can be seen in the frequent disturbances of the relation between daughter-in-law and mother-in-law. If the man is mainly valued because his conquest is a triumph over another woman, she may lose interest in him as soon as success has been achieved. The attitude towards the rival woman then implies: 'You (standing for the mother) had that wonderful breast which I could not get when you withheld it from me and which I still wish to rob you of; therefore I take from you that penis which you cherish.' The need to repeat this triumph over a hated rival often strongly contributes to the search for another and yet another man.

When hate and envy of the mother are not so strong, nevertheless disappointment and grievance may lead to a turning away from her; but an idealization of the second object, the father's penis and the father, may then be more successful. This idealization derives mainly from the search for a good object, a search which has not succeeded in the first place and therefore may fail again, but need not fail if the love for the father is dominant in the jealousy situation; for then the woman can combine some hatred against the mother and love for the father and later on for other men. In this case friendly emotions towards women are possible, as long as they do not too much represent a mother substitute. Friendship with women and homosexuality may then be based on the need to find a good object instead of the avoided primal object. The fact that such people—and this applies to men as well as to women—can have good object relations is therefore often deceptive. The underlying envy towards the primal object is split off but remains operative and is liable to disturb any relations.

In a number of cases I found that frigidity, occurring in different degrees, was a result of unstable attitudes to the penis, based mainly on a flight from the primal object. The capacity for full oral gratification, which is rooted in a satisfactory relation to the mother, is the basis for experiencing full genital orgasm (Freud).

In men, the envy of the mother's breast is also a very important factor. If it is strong and oral gratification thereby impaired, hatred and anxieties are transferred to the vagina. Whereas normally the genital development enables the boy to retain his mother as a love-object, a deep disturbance in the oral relation opens the way for severe difficulties in the genital attitude towards women. The consequence of a disturbed relation first to the breast and then to the vagina are manifold, such as impairment of genital potency, compulsive need for genital gratification, promiscuity, and homosexuality.

It appears that one source of guilt about homosexuality is the feeling of having turned away with hate from the mother and betrayed her by making an ally of the father's penis and of the father. Both during the Oedipus stage and in later life this element of betrayal of a loved woman may have repercussions, such as a disturbance in friendships with men, even if they are not of a manifest homosexual nature. On the other hand, I have observed that the guilt towards a loved woman and the anxiety implied in that attitude often reinforce the flight from her and increase homosexual tendencies.

Excessive envy of the breast is likely to extend to all

feminine attributes, in particular to the woman's capacity to bear children. If development is successful, the man derives compensation for these unfulfilled feminine desires by a good relation to his wife or lover and by becoming the father of the children she bears him. This relation opens up experiences such as identification with his child which in many ways make up for early envy and frustrations; also the feeling that he has created the child counteracts the man's early envy of the mother's femininity.

In both male and female envy plays a part in the desire to take away the attributes of the other sex, as well as to possess or spoil those of the parent of the same sex. It follows that paranoid jealousy and rivalry in the direct and inverted Oedipus situation are in both sexes, however divergent their development, based on excessive envy towards the primal object, the mother, or rather her breast.

III

The 'good' breast that feeds and initiates the love relation to the mother is the representative of the life instinct[1] and is also felt as the first manifestation of creativeness. In this fundamental relation the infant receives not only the gratification he desires but feels that he is being kept alive. For hunger, which rouses the fear of starvation—possibly even all physical and mental pain—is felt as the threat of death. If the identification with a good and life-giving internalized object can be maintained, this becomes an impetus towards creativeness. Though superficially this may manifest itself as a coveting of the prestige, wealth, and power which others have attained,[2] its actual aim is creativeness.

---

[1] *Developments in Psycho-Analysis*, Chapters VI and VII.
[2] 'On Identification' (*New Directions in Psycho-Analysis*).

D

The capacity to give and to preserve life is felt as the greatest gift and therefore creativeness becomes the deepest cause for envy. The spoiling of creativity implied in envy is illustrated in Milton's *Paradise Lost*[1] where Satan, envious of God, decides to become the usurper of Heaven. He makes war on God in his attempt to spoil the heavenly life and falls out of Heaven. Fallen, he and his other fallen angels build Hell as a rival to Heaven, and become the destructive force which attempts to destroy what God creates.[2] This theological idea seems to come down from St Augustine, who describes Life as a creative force opposed to Envy, a destructive force. In this connection, the First Letter to the Corinthians reads, 'Love envieth not'.

My psycho-analytic experience has shown me that envy of creativeness is a fundamental element in the disturbance of the creative process. To spoil and destroy the initial source of goodness soon leads to destroying and attacking the babies that the mother contains and results in the good object being turned into a hostile, critical, and envious one. The super-ego figure on which strong envy has been projected becomes particularly persecutory and interferes with thought processes and with every productive activity, ultimately with creativeness.

The envious and destructive attitude towards the breast underlies destructive criticism which is often described as 'biting' and 'pernicious'. It is particularly creativeness which becomes the object of such attacks. Thus Spenser in 'The Faerie Queene' describes envy as a ravenous wolf:

[1] Books I and II.

[2] But by the envy of the devil, death entered into the world, and they that are of his portion make trial thereof. (Wisdom of Solomon, Ch. 3, v. 24.)

He hated all good workes and vertuous deeds

.   .   .   .

And eke the verse of famous Poets witt
He does backebite, and spightfull poison spues[1]
From leprous mouth on all that ever writt.

Constructive criticism has different sources; it aims at helping the other person and furthering his work. Sometimes it derives from a strong identification with the person whose work is under discussion. Maternal or fatherly attitudes may also enter, and often a confidence in one's own creativeness counteracts envy.

A particular cause of envy is the relative absence of it in others. The envied person is felt to possess what is at bottom most prized and desired—and this is a good object, which also implies a good character and sanity. Moreover, the person who can ungrudgingly enjoy other people's creative work and happiness is spared the torments of envy, grievance, and persecution. Whereas envy is a source of great unhappiness, a relative freedom from it is felt to underlie contented and peaceful states of mind—ultimately sanity. This is also in fact the basis of inner resources and resilience which can be observed in people who, even after great adversity and mental pain, regain their peace of mind.

---

[1] In Chaucer also we find extensive references to this backbiting and destructive criticising which characterizes the envious person. He describes the sin of backbiting as arising from a compound of the envious person's unhappiness at other men's goodness and prosperity, and his joy in their harm. The sinful behaviour is characterized by 'the man who praises his neighbour but with wicked intent, for he always put "but" at the end, and follows it with another of greater blame than is the worth of the person. Or, if a man is good and does or says things of good intent, the backbiter will turn all this goodness upside down to his own shrewd intent. Or if other men speak good of a man, then the backbiter will say that he is very good, but will point to someone else who is better, and will thus disparage he whom other men praise.'

Such an attitude, which includes gratitude for pleasures of the past and enjoyment of what the present can give, expresses itself in serenity. In old people, it makes possible the adaptation to the knowledge that youth cannot be regained and enables them to take pleasure and interest in the lives of young people. The well-known fact that parents relive in their children and grand-children their own lives —if this is not an expression of excessive possessiveness and deflected ambition—illustrates what I am trying to convey. Those who feel that they have had a share in the experience and pleasures of life are much more able to believe in the continuity of life.[1] Such capacity for resignation without undue bitterness and yet keeping the power of enjoyment alive has its roots in infancy and depends on how far the baby had been able to enjoy the breast without excessively envying the mother for its possession. I suggest that the happiness experienced in infancy and the love for the good object which enriches the personality underlie the capacity for enjoyment and sublimation, and still make themselves felt in old age. When Goethe said, 'He is the happiest of men who can make the end of his life agree closely with the beginning', I would interpret 'the beginning' as the early happy relation to the mother which throughout life mitigates hate and anxiety and still gives the old person support and contentment. An infant who has securely established the good object can also find compensations for loss and deprivation in adult life. All this is felt by the envious person as something he can never attain because he can never be satisfied, and therefore his envy is reinforced.

---

[1] The belief in the continuity of life was significantly expressed in the remark of a boy in his fifth year whose mother was pregnant. He expressed the hope that the expected baby would be a girl, and added, 'then she will have babies, and her babies will have babies, and then it goes on forever'.

CHAPTER FIVE

I

I SHALL now illustrate some of my conclusions by clinical material.[1] My first instance is taken from the analysis of a woman patient. She had been breast fed, but circumstances had otherwise not been favourable and she was convinced that her babyhood and feeding had been wholly unsatisfactory. Her grievance about the past linked with hopelessness about the present and future. Envy of the feeding breast, and the ensuing difficulties in object relations, had already been extensively analysed prior to the material to which I am going to refer.

The patient telephoned and said that she could not come for treatment because of a pain in her shoulder. On the next day she rang me to say that she was still not well but expected to see me on the following day. When, on the third day, she actually came, she was full of complaints. She had been looked after by her maid, but nobody else had taken an interest in her. She described to me that at one moment her pain had suddenly increased, together with a sense of extreme coldness. She had felt an impetuous need for somebody to come at once and cover up her shoulder,

[1] I am aware that in the following case material details of the patient's history, personality, age, and external circumstances would have been of value. Reasons of discretion make it impossible to go into such details and I can only attempt illustrations of my main themes by extracts from material.

so that it should get warm, and to go away again as soon as that was done. At that instant it occurred to her that this must be how she had felt as a baby when she wanted to be looked after and nobody came.

It was characteristic of the patient's attitude to people, and threw light on her earliest relation to the breast, that she desired to be looked after but at the same time repelled the very object which was to gratify her. The suspicion of the gift received, together with her impetuous need to be cared for, which ultimately meant a desire to be fed, expressed her ambivalent attitude towards the breast. I have referred to infants whose response to frustration is to make insufficient use of the gratification that the feed, even if delayed, could give them. I would surmise that though they do not give up their desires for a gratifying breast, they cannot enjoy it and therefore repel it. The case under discussion illustrates some of the reasons for this attitude: suspicion of the gift she wished to receive because the object was already spoilt by envy and hatred, and at the same time deep resentment about every frustration. We also have to remember—and this applies to other adults in whom envy is marked—that many disappointing experiences, no doubt partly due to her own attitude, had contributed to her feeling that the desired care would not be satisfactory.

In the course of this session the patient reported a dream: she was in a restaurant, seated at a table; however nobody came to serve her. She decided to join a queue and fetch herself something to eat. In front of her was a woman who took two or three little cakes and went away with them. The patient also took two or three little cakes. From her associations I am selecting the following: the woman seemed very determined, and her figure was reminiscent of mine. There was a sudden doubt about the name of the cakes (actually *petits fours*) which she first thought were 'petit fru', which reminded her of 'petit frau' and thus of 'Frau Klein'. The gist of my interpretations was that her grievance about the missed analytic sessions related to the unsatisfactory feeds and unhappiness in babyhood. The two cakes out of the 'two or three' stood for the breast which she felt she had been twice deprived of by missing analytic sessions. There were 'two or three' because she was not sure whether she would be able to come on the third day. The fact that the woman was 'determined' and that the patient followed her example in taking the cakes pointed both at her identification with the analyst and at projection of her own greed on to her. In the context of this book, one aspect of the dream is most relevant. The analyst who went away with the two or three *petits fours* stood not only for the breast which was withheld, but also for the breast which was going to *feed itself*. (Taken together with other material, the 'determined' analyst did not only represent a breast but a person with whose qualities, good and bad, the patient identified herself.)

To frustration had thus been added envy of the breast. This envy had given rise to bitter resentment, for the mother had been felt to be selfish and mean, feeding and loving herself rather than her baby. In the analytic situation I was suspected of having enjoyed myself during the time when she was absent, or of having given the time to other patients whom I preferred. The queue which the patient had decided to join referred to other more favoured rivals.

The response to the analysis of the dream was a striking change in the emotional situation. The patient now experienced a feeling of happiness and gratitude more vividly than in previous analytic sessions. She had tears in her eyes, which was unusual, and said that she felt as if she now had

had an entirely satisfactory feed.[1] It also occurred to her
that her breast-feeding and her infancy might have been
happier than she had assumed. Also, she felt more hopeful
about the future and the result of her analysis. The patient
had more fully realized one part of herself, which was by
no means unknown to her in other connections. She was
aware that she was envious and jealous of various people but
had not been able to recognize it sufficiently in the relation
to the analyst because it was too painful to experience that
she was envying and spoiling the analyst as well as the success of the analysis. In this session, after the interpretations
referred to, her envy had lessened; the capacity for enjoyment and gratitude had come to the fore, and she was able
to experience the analytic session as a happy feed. This emotional situation had to be worked through over and over
again, both in the positive and negative transference, until a
more stable result was achieved.

It was by enabling her gradually to bring the split-off
parts of her self together in relation to the analyst, and by
her recognizing how envious and therefore suspicious she
was of me, and in the first place of her mother, that the
experience of that happy feed came about. This was bound
up with feelings of gratitude. In the course of the analysis
envy was diminished and feelings of gratitude became much
more frequent and lasting.

[1] It is not only in children but also in adults that a full revival of the emotions felt during the earliest feeding experiences can come about in the transference situation. For instance, a feeling of hunger or thirst comes up very
strongly during the session and has gone after the interpretation which was
felt to have satisfied it. One of my patients, overcome by such feelings, got
up from the couch and put his arms round one section of the arch which
separated one part of my consulting room from the other. I have repeatedly
heard the expression at the end of such sessions 'I have been well nourished'.
The good object, in its earliest primitive form as the mother who takes care
of the baby and feeds him, had been regained.

II

My second instance is taken from the analysis of a woman patient with strong depressive and schizoid features. She had suffered from depressive states over a long period. The analysis proceeded and made some headway, though the patient again and again expressed her doubts about the work. I had interpreted the destructive impulses against the analyst, parents, and siblings, and the analysis succeeded in making her recognize specific phantasies of destructive attacks on her mother's body. Such insight was usually followed by depression but not of an unmanageable nature.

It is remarkable that during the early part of her treatment the depth and severity of the patient's difficulties could not be seen. Socially, she gave an impression of being a pleasant person, though liable to be depressed. Her reparative tendencies and helpful attitude towards friends were quite genuine. However, the severity of her illness became apparent at one stage, partly due to the previous analytic work and partly to some external experiences. Several disappointments occurred; but it was an unexpected success in her professional career that brought more to the fore what I had been analysing for some years, namely, the intense rivalry with me and a feeling that she might in her own field become equal, or rather superior, to me. Both she and I came to recognize the importance of her destructive envy towards me; and, as always when we reach these deep strata, it appeared that whatever destructive impulses were there, they were felt to be omnipotent and therefore irrevocable and irremediable. I had until then analysed her oral-sadistic desires extensively, and that is also how we arrived at her partial realization of her destructive impulses towards her mother and myself. The analysis had also dealt with urethral- and anal-sadistic desires, but in this respect I felt that I had not made much headway and that her understanding of these impulses and phantasies was more of an intellectual nature. During the particular period I now want to discuss, urethral material appeared with increased strength.

A feeling of great elation about her success soon developed and was ushered in by a dream which showed the triumph over me and, underlying this, the destructive envy of me standing for her mother. In the dream she was up in the air on a magic carpet which supported her and was above the top of a tree. She was sufficiently high up to look through a window into a room where a cow was munching something which appeared to be an endless strip of blanket. In the same night she also had a bit of a dream in which her pants were wet.

The associations to this dream made it clear that being on top of the tree meant having outstripped me, for the cow represented myself, at whom she looked with contempt. Quite early on in her analysis she had had a dream in which I was represented by an apathetic cow-like woman, whereas she was a little girl who made a brilliant and successful speech. My interpretations at that time that she had made the analyst into a contemptible person, whereas she gave such a successful performance in spite of being so much younger, had only partly been accepted although she fully realized that the little girl was herself and the cow-woman was the analyst. This dream led gradually to a stronger realization of her destructive and envious attacks upon me and her mother. Ever since, the cow-woman, standing for myself, had been a well-established feature in the material, and therefore it was quite clear that in the new dream the cow in the room into which she was looking was the analyst. She associated that the endless strip of blanket represented an endless stream of words, and it occurred to her that these were all the words I had ever said in the analysis and which I now had to swallow. The strip of blanket was a hit at the woolliness and worthlessness of my interpretations. Here we see the full devaluation of the primal object, significantly represented by the cow, as well as the grievance against the mother who had not fed her satisfactorily. The punishment inflicted on me by having to eat all my words throws light on the deep distrust and the doubts which had again and again assailed her in the course of the analysis. It became quite clear after my interpretations that the ill-treated analyst could not be trusted, and that she could also have no confidence in the devalued analysis. The patient was surprised and shocked at her attitude towards me, which prior to the dream she had for a long time refused to acknowledge in its full impact.

The wet pants in the dream and the association to them expressed (among other meanings) poisonous urethral attacks on the analyst which were to destroy her mental powers and change her into the cow-woman. Very soon she had another dream illustrating this particular point. She was standing at the bottom of a staircase, looking up at a young couple with whom something was very wrong. She threw a woollen ball up to them, which she herself described as 'good magic', and her associations showed that bad magic, and more specifically poison, must have given rise to the need to use good magic afterwards. The associations to the couple enabled me to interpret a strongly denied current jealousy situation and led us from the present back to earlier experiences, ultimate of course to the parents. The destructive and envious feelings towards the analyst, and in the past towards her mother, turned out to underlie the jealousy and envy towards the couple in the dream. The fact that this light ball never reached the couple implied that her reparation did not succeed; and the anxiety about such failure was an important element in her depression.

This is only an extract from the material which convincingly proved to the patient her poisonous envy of the analyst and of her primal object. She succumbed to depression of a depth such as she had never had before. The main cause of this depression, which followed on her state of elation, was that she had been made to realize a completely split-off part of herself which so far she had been unable to acknowledge. As I said earlier, it was very difficult to help her to realize her hate and aggressiveness. But when we came to this particular source of destructiveness, her envy as the impetus towards damaging and humiliating the analyst, whom in another part of her mind she highly valued, she could not bear to see herself in that light. She did not appear to be particularly boastful or conceited, but by means of a variety of splitting processes and manic defences she had clung to an idealized picture of herself. As a consequence of the realization, which at that stage of the analysis she could no longer deny, that she felt bad and despicable, the idealization broke down and distrust of herself as well as guilt about irrevocable harm done in the past and in the present came up. Her guilt and depression focused on her feeling of ingratitude towards the analyst who, she knew, had helped her and was helping her, and towards whom she felt contempt and hate: ultimately on the ingratitude towards her mother, whom she unconsciously saw as spoilt and damaged by her envy and destructive impulses.

The analysis of her depression led to an improvement which after some months was followed by a renewed deep depression. This was caused by the patient recognizing more fully her virulent anal-sadistic attacks on the analyst, and in the past on her family, and confirmed her feeling both of illness and of badness. It was the first time that she was able to see how strongly urethral- and anal-sadistic features had been split off. Each of these had involved important parts of the patient's personality and interests. The steps towards integration which took place following the analysis of the depression implied regaining these lost parts, and the necessity to face them was the cause of her depression.

III

The next instance is of a woman patient whom I would describe as fairly normal. She had in the course of time become more and more aware of envy experienced both towards an older sister and towards her mother. The envy of the sister had been counteracted by a feeling of strong intellectual superiority which had a basis in fact, and by an unconscious feeling that the sister was extremely neurotic. The envy of the mother was counteracted by very strong feelings of love and appreciation of her goodness.

The patient reported a dream in which she was alone in a railway carriage with a woman, of whom she could only see the back, who was leaning towards the door of the compartment in great danger of falling out. The patient held her strongly, grasping her by the belt with one hand; with the other hand she wrote a notice to the effect that a doctor was engaged with a patient in this compartment and should not be disturbed, and she put up this notice on the window.

From the associations to the dream I select the following: the patient had a strong feeling that the figure on whom she kept a tight grip was part of herself, and a mad one. In the dream she had a conviction that she should not let her fall out through the door but should keep her in the compartment and deal with her. The analysis of the dream revealed that the compartment stood for herself. The associations to the hair, which was only seen from behind, were to the older sister. Further associations led to recognition of rivalry and envy in relation to her, going back to the time when the patient was still a child, while her sister was already being courted. She then spoke of a dress which her mother wore and which as a child the patient had both admired and coveted. This dress had very clearly shown the shape of the breasts, and it became more evident than ever before, though none of this was entirely new, that what she originally envied and spoiled in her phantasy was the mother's breast.

This recognition gave rise to increased feelings of guilt, both towards her sister and her mother, and led to a further revision of her earliest relations. She arrived at a much more compassionate understanding of the deficiencies of this sister and felt that she had not loved her sufficiently. She also discovered that she had loved her in her early childhood more than she had remembered.

I interpreted that the patient felt that she had to keep a grip on a mad, split-off part of herself, which was also linked with the internalization of the neurotic sister. Following the interpretation of the dream, the patient, who had reasons for regarding herself as fairly normal, had a feeling of strong surprise and shock. This case illustrates a conclusion that is becoming increasingly familiar, namely, that a residue of paranoid and schizoid feelings and mechanisms, often split-off from the other parts of the self, exists even in normal people.[1]

The patient's feeling that she had to keep a firm hold on

---

[1] Freud's *Interpretation of Dreams* shows clearly that some of this residue of madness finds expression in dreams, and that they are therefore a most valuable safeguard for sanity.

that figure implied that she should also have helped her sister more, prevented her, as it were, from falling; and this feeling was now re-experienced in connection with her as an internalized object. The revision of her earliest relations was bound up with changes in feelings towards her primal introjected objects. The fact that her sister also represented the mad part of herself turned out to be partly a projection of her own schizoid and paranoid feelings on to her sister. It was together with this realization that the split in her ego diminished.

IV

I now wish to refer to a man patient and report a dream which had a strong effect in making him recognize not only destructive impulses towards the analyst and towards his mother, but envy as a very specific factor in his relation to them. Up till then, and with strong feelings of guilt, he had already recognized in some measure his destructive impulses, but still did not realize envious and hostile feelings directed against the creativeness of the analyst, and of his mother in the past. He was aware, though, that he experienced envy towards other people and that, together with a good relation to his father, he had also feelings of rivalry and jealousy. The following dream brought a much stronger insight into his envy of the analyst and threw light on his early desires to possess all the feminine attributes of his mother.

In the dream the patient had been fishing; he was wondering whether he should kill the fish he caught in order to eat it, but decided to put it into a basket and let it die. The basket in which he was carrying the fish was a woman's laundry basket. The fish suddenly turned into a beautiful baby and there was something green about the baby's clothes. Then he noticed—and at that point he became very concerned—that the baby's intestines were protruding because it had been damaged by the hook which it had swallowed in its fish state. The association to green was the cover of the books in the *International Psycho-Analytical Library*, and the patient remarked that the fish in the basket stood for one of my books which he had obviously stolen. Further associations, however, showed that the fish was not only my work and my baby but also stood for myself. My swallowing the hook, which meant having swallowed the bait, expressed his feeling that I had thought better of him than he deserved and not recognized that there were also very destructive parts of his self operative in relation to me. Although the patient still could not fully acknowledge that the way he treated the fish, the baby, and myself meant destroying me and my work out of envy, he unconsciously realized it. I also interpreted that the laundry basket in this connection expressed his desire to be a woman, to have babies, and deprive his mother of them. The effect of this step in integration was a strong onset of depression due to his having to face the aggressive components of his personality. Although this had been foreshadowed in the earlier part of his analysis, he now experienced it as a shock and as horror of himself.

The following night the patient dreamed of a pike, to which he associated whales and sharks, but he did not feel in the dream that the pike was a dangerous creature. It was old and looked tired and very worn. On it was a suckerfish, and he at once suggested that the suckerfish does not suck the pike or the whale but sucks itself on to its surface and is thus protected from attacks by other fish. The patient recognized that this explanation was a defence against the feeling that he was the suckerfish and I was the old and worn-out pike and was in that state because I had been so badly treated in the dream of the previous night, and because he felt I had been sucked dry by him. This had made me not only into an injured but also into a dangerous object. In other words, persecutory as well as depressive anxiety had come to the fore; the pike associated to whales and sharks showed the persecutory aspects, whereas its old and worn-out appearance expressed the patient's sense of guilt about the harm he felt he had been doing and was doing to me.

The strong depression which followed this insight lasted for several weeks, more or less uninterrupted, but did not interfere with the patient's work and family life. He described this depression as different from any he had experienced formerly and much deeper. The urge for reparation, expressed in physical and mental work, was increased by the depression and paved the way to an overcoming of it. The result of this phase in the analysis was very noticeable. Even when the depression had lifted after having been worked through, the patient was convinced that he would never see himself again in the way he had done before, though this no longer implied a feeling of dejection but a greater knowledge of himself as well as greater tolerance of other people. What the analysis had achieved was an important step in integration, bound up with the patient being capable of facing his psychic reality. In the course of his analysis, however, there were times when this attitude could not be maintained. That is to say, as in every case, the working-through was a gradual process.

Although his observation and judgment of people had previously been fairly normal, there was definite improvement as a result of this stage of his treatment. A further consequence was that memories of childhood and attitude to siblings came up with greater strength and led back to

E

the early relation to the mother. During the state of depression I have referred to, he had, as he recognized, lost to a large extent the pleasure and interest in the analysis; but he regained them completely when the depression lifted. He soon brought a dream which he himself saw as mildly belittling the analyst, but which turned out in the analysis to express strong devaluation. In the dream he had to deal with a delinquent boy, but was not satisfied with the way in which he had handled the situation. The boy's father suggested taking the patient by car to his destination. He noticed that he was being taken further and further away from where he wanted to go. After a while he thanked the father and got out of the car; but he was not lost because he kept, as usual, a general sense of direction. In passing, he looked at a rather extraordinary building which, he thought, looked interesting and suitable for an exhibition but would not be pleasant to live in. His associations to it linked with some aspect of my appearance. Then he spoke of that building having two wings and remembered the expression 'taking somebody under one's wing'. He recognized that the delinquent boy in whom he had taken an interest stood for himself and the continuation of the dream showed why he was delinquent: when the father, representing the analyst, was taking him more and more away from his destination, this expressed doubts he made use of partly in order to devalue me; he queried whether I was taking him in the right direction, whether it was necessary to go so deep, and whether I was doing harm to him. When he referred to his keeping a sense of direction and to his not feeling lost, this implied the contrary of the accusations against the boy's father (the analyst): he knew that the analysis was very valuable to him and that it was his envy of me which increased his doubts.

He also understood that the interesting building, which

he would not like to live in, represented the analyst. On the other hand, he felt that by analysing him I had taken him under my wing and was protecting him against his conflicts and anxieties. The doubts and the accusations against me in the dream were used as devaluation and related not only to envy but also to despondency about the envy and to his feelings of guilt because of his ingratitude.

There was another interpretation of this dream, which was also confirmed by later ones, and which was based on the fact that in the analytic situation I often stood for the father, changing quickly into the mother, and at times representing both parents simultaneously. This interpretation was that the accusation against the father for taking him in the wrong direction was linked with his early homosexual attraction towards the father. This attraction had proved during the analysis to be bound up with intense feelings of guilt, because I was able to show the patient that the strongly split-off envy and hatred of his mother and her breast had contributed to his turning towards the father, and that his homosexual desires were felt to be a hostile alliance against the mother. The accusation that the father took him in the wrong direction linked with the general feeling we so often find in patients that he had been seduced into homosexuality. Here we have the projection of the individual's own desires on to the parent.

The analysis of his sense of guilt had various effects; he experienced a deeper love for his parents; he also realized —and these two facts are closely linked—that there had been a compulsive element in his need to make reparation. An over-strong identification with the object harmed in phantasy—originally the mother—had impaired his capacity for full enjoyment and thereby to some extent impoverished his life. It became clear that even in his earliest relation to his mother, though there was no reason to doubt that he had been happy in the suckling situation, he had not been able to enjoy it completely because of his fear of exhausting or depriving the breast. On the other hand, the interference with his enjoyment gave cause for grievance and increased his feelings of persecution. This is an instance of the process I described in a previous section by which in the early stages of development guilt—in particular guilt about destructive envy of the mother and the analyst—is liable to change into persecution. Through the analysis of primary envy and a corresponding lessening of depressive and persecutory anxiety, his capacity for enjoyment and gratitude at a deep level increased.

v

I shall now mention the case of another man patient in whom a tendency to depression also went with a compulsive need for reparation; his ambition, rivalry, and envy, co-existing with many good character traits, had been gradually analysed. Nevertheless, it took some years[1] until the envy of the breast and of its creativeness and the desire to spoil it, which was very much split off, were fully experienced by the patient. Early on in his analysis he had a dream that he described as 'ludicrous': he was smoking his pipe and it was filled with my papers which had been torn out of one of my books. He first expressed great surprise about this because 'one does not smoke printed papers'. I interpreted that this was only a minor feature of the

[1] Experience has shown me that when the analyst becomes fully convinced of the importance of a new aspect of emotional life, he becomes able to interpret it earlier in the analysis. By thus giving it sufficient emphasis whenever the material allows it, he may bring the patient much sooner to the realization of such processes and in this way the effectiveness of the analysis may be enhanced.

dream; the main meaning was that he had torn up my work and was destroying it. I also pointed out that the destruction of my papers was of an anal-sadistic nature, implied in smoking them. He had denied these aggressive attacks; for, together with the strength of his splitting processes, he had a great capacity for denial. Another aspect of this dream was that persecutory feelings came up in connection with the analysis. Previous interpretations had been resented and felt as something which he had to 'put into his pipe and smoke'. The analysis of his dream helped the patient to recognize his destructive impulses against the analyst, and also that they had been stimulated by a jealousy situation which had arisen on the previous day; it centred on the feeling that somebody else was more valued by me than himself. But the insight gained did not lead to an understanding of his envy of the analyst, though it was interpreted to him. I have no doubt, however, that this paved the way for material in which destructive impulses and envy gradually became more and more clear.

A climax was reached at a later stage in his analysis when all these feelings in relation to the analyst came home to the patient in full force. The patient reported a dream which once again he described as 'ludicrous': he was moving along with great speed, as if in a motor car. He was standing on a semi-circular contraption which was made either out of wire or some 'atomic stuff'. As he put it, 'this kept me going'. Suddenly he noticed that the thing he was standing on was falling to pieces, and he was much distressed. He associated to the semi-circular object the breast and the erection of the penis, implying his potency. His sense of guilt about not making the right use of his analysis and about his destructive impulses towards me entered into this dream. He felt in his depression that I could not be preserved and there were many links to similar anxieties, partly even conscious, that he had not been able to protect his mother when his father was away during the war and later on. His feeling of guilt in relation to his mother and to myself had been extensively analysed by then. But recently he had come more specifically to feel that it was his envy that was destructive of me. His feelings of guilt and unhappiness were all the greater because in one part of his mind he was grateful to the analyst. The phrase 'this kept me going' implied how essential the analysis was to him and that it was a pre-condition for his potency in the widest sense, that is to say for the success of all his aspirations.

The realization of his envy and hate towards me came as a shock and was followed by strong depression and a feeling of unworthiness. I believe that this kind of shock, which I have now reported in several cases, is the result of an important step in the healing of the split between parts of the self, and thus a stage of progress in ego-integration.

A still fuller realization of his ambition and envy came in a session following the second dream. He spoke of his knowing his limitations and, as he put it, he did not expect that he would cover himself and his profession with glory. At this moment, and still under the influence of the dream, he understood that this way of putting it showed the strength of his ambition and his envious comparison with me. After an initial feeling of surprise, this recognition carried full conviction.

CHAPTER SIX

I

I HAVE often described my approach to anxiety as a focal point of my technique. However, from the very beginning, anxieties cannot be encountered without the defences against them. As I pointed out in an earlier section, the first and foremost function of the ego is to deal with anxiety. I even think it is likely that the primordial anxiety, engendered by the threat of the death instinct within, might be the explanation why the ego is brought into activity from birth onwards. The ego is constantly protecting itself against the pain and tension to which anxiety gives rise, and therefore makes use of defences from the beginning of post-natal life. I have for many years held the view that the greater or lesser capacity of the ego to bear anxiety is a constitutional factor that strongly influences the development of defences. If its capacity to cope with anxiety is inadequate, the ego may return regressively to earlier defences, or even be driven to the excessive use of those appropriate to its stage. As a result, persecutory anxiety and the methods of dealing with it can be so strong that subsequently the working-through of the depressive position is impaired. In some cases, particularly of a psychotic type, we are confronted from the beginning with defences of such an apparently impenetrable nature that it may for some time seem impossible to analyse them.

I shall now enumerate some of the defences against envy that I have encountered in the course of my work. Some of the earliest defences often described before, such as omnipotence, denial, and splitting, are reinforced by envy. In an early section I have suggested that *idealization* not only serves as a defence against persecution but also against envy. In infants, if the normal splitting between the good and the bad object does not initially succeed, this failure, bound up with excessive envy, often results in splitting between an omnipotently idealized and a very bad primal object. Strongly exalting the object and its gifts is an attempt to diminish envy. However, if envy is very strong, it is likely, sooner or later, to turn against the primal idealized object and against other people who, in the course of development, come to stand for it.

As suggested earlier, when the fundamental normal splitting into love and hate and into the good and the bad object is not successful, *confusion* between the good and bad object may arise.[1] I believe this to be the basis of any confusion—whether in severe confusional states or in milder forms such as indecision—namely a difficulty in coming to conclusions and a disturbed capacity for clear thinking. But confusion is also used defensively: this can be seen on all levels of development. By becoming confused as to whether a substitute for the original figure is good or bad, persecution as well as the guilt about spoiling and attacking the primary object by envy is to some extent counteracted. The fight against envy takes on another character when, together with the depressive position, several feelings of guilt set in. Even with people in whom envy is not excessive, the concern for the object, the identification with it, and the fear of its loss and of the harm

[1] Cf. Rosenfeld, 'Note on the Psychopathology of Confusional States in Chronic Schizophrenias' (1950).

done to its creativeness, is an important factor in the difficulty of working through the depressive position.

The *flight from the mother to other people*, who are admired
and idealized in order to avoid hostile feelings towards that
most important envied (and therefore hated) object, the
breast, becomes also a means of preserving the breast—
which means also preserving the mother.[1] I have often
pointed out that the way in which the turning from the
first to the second object, the father, is carried out is of
major importance. If envy and hatred are predominant,
these emotions are to some degree transferred to the father
or to siblings, and later to other people, and thereafter the
flight mechanism fails.

Bound up with the turning away from the primal object
is dispersal of the feeling towards it which, at a later stage
of development, might lead to promiscuity. The widening
of object relations in infancy is a normal process. In so far
as the relation to new objects is in some part a substitute
for love for the mother, and not predominantly a flight
from the hate of her, the new objects are helpful, and a
compensation for the unavoidable feeling of loss of the unique
first object—a loss arising with the depressive position.
Love and gratitude are then in varying degrees preserved
in the new relations, though these emotions are to some
extent cut off from the feelings towards the mother. However, if the dispersal of emotions is predominantly used as
a defence against envy and hatred, such defences are not a
basis for stable object relations because they are influenced
by the persistent hostility to the first object.

Defence against envy often takes the form of *devaluation
of the object*. I have suggested that spoiling and devaluing are
inherent in envy. The object which has been devalued need

[1] Cf. Chapter VI in *Developments in Psycho-Analysis*.

not be envied any more. This soon applies to the idealized object, which is devalued and therefore no longer idealized. How quickly this idealization breaks down depends on the strength of envy. But devaluation and ingratitude are resorted to at every level of development as defences against envy, and in some people remain characteristic of their object relations. I have referred to those patients who, in the transference situation, after having been decidedly helped by an interpretation, criticize it, until at last nothing good is left of it. To give an instance: a patient, who during an analytic session had arrived at a satisfactory solution of an external problem, started the next session by saying that he felt very annoyed with me: I had roused great anxiety on the previous day in making him face this particular problem. It also appeared that he felt accused and devalued by me because, until the problem was analysed, the solution had not occurred to him. It was only on reflection that he acknowledged that the analysis had actually been helpful.

A defence particular to more depressive types is *devaluation of the self*. Some people may be unable to develop their gifts and use them in a successful way. In other cases this attitude only comes up on certain occasions, whenever there is danger of rivalry with an important figure. By devaluing their own gifts they both deny envy and punish themselves for it. In analysis it can be seen, however, that devaluation of the self again stirs up envy of the analyst, who is felt to be superior, particularly because the patient has strongly devalued himself. Depriving oneself of success has, of course, many determinants, and this applies to all the attitudes I am referring to.[1] But I found as one of the deepest roots of this defence the guilt and unhappiness

[1] Cf. Freud, 'Some Character-Types Met with in Psycho-Analytic Work' (1915).

about not having been able to preserve the good object because of envy. People who have rather precariously established their good object suffer under anxiety lest it be spoilt and lost by competitive and envious feelings, and therefore have to avoid success and competition.

Another defence against envy is closely linked with greed. By *internalizing the breast so greedily* that in the infant's mind it becomes entirely his possession and controlled by him, he feels that all the good that he attributes to it will be his own. This is used to counteract envy. It is the very greed with which this internalization is carried out that contains the germ of failure. As I said earlier, a good object which is well established, and therefore assimilated, not only loves the subject but is loved by it. This, I believe, is characteristic of the relation to a good object, but does not apply, or only in a minor degree, to an idealized one. By powerful and violent possessiveness, the good object is felt to turn into a destroyed persecutor and the consequences of envy are not sufficiently prevented. By contrast, if tolerance towards a loved person is experienced, it is also projected on to others, who thus become friendly figures.

A frequent method of defence is *to stir up envy in others* by one's own success, possessions, and good fortune, thereby reversing the situation in which envy is experienced. The ineffectiveness of this method derives from the persecutory anxiety to which it gives rise. Envious people, and in particular the envious internal object, are felt to be the worst persecutors. Another reason why this defence is precarious derives ultimately from the depressive position. The desire to make other people, particularly loved ones, envious and to triumph over them gives rise to guilt and to the fear of harming them. The anxiety stirred up impairs the enjoyment of one's own possessions and again increases envy.

There is another, and not infrequent defence, the *stifling of feelings of love and the corresponding intensifying of hate*, because this is less painful than to bear the guilt arising from the combination of love, hate, and envy. This may not express itself as hate but takes on the appearance of indifference. An allied defence is to withdraw from contact with people. The need for independence, which, as we know, is a normal phenomenon of development, may be reinforced in order to avoid gratitude or guilt about ingratitude and envy. In analysis, we find that unconsciously this independence is actually quite spurious: the individual remains dependent on his internal object.

Herbert Rosenfeld[1] has described a particular method of dealing with the situation when split-off parts of the personality, including the most envious and destructive parts, come together, and steps in integration occur. He showed that 'acting out' is used in order to avoid the undoing of the split; in my view *acting out* in so far as it is used to avoid integration, becomes a defence against the anxieties aroused by accepting the envious part of the self.

I have by no means described all the defences against envy because their variety is infinite. They are closely interlinked with the defences against destructive impulses and persecutory and depressive anxiety. How successful they are depends on many external and internal factors. As has been mentioned, when envy is strong, and therefore likely to reappear in all object relations, defences against it seem to be precarious; those against destructive impulses not dominated by envy appear to be much more effective, though they might imply inhibitions and limitations of the personality.

[1] 'An Investigation of the Need of Neurotic and Psychotic Patients to Act Out during Analysis' (1955).

When schizoid and paranoid features are in the ascendant, defences against envy cannot be successful, for the attacks on the subject lead to an increased feeling of persecution that can only be dealt with by renewed attacks, that is to say, by reinforcing the destructive impulses. In this way is set up a vicious circle that impairs the ability to counteract envy. This applies particularly to schizophrenic cases and explains to some extent the difficulties in the way of curing them.[1]

The outcome is more favourable when, in some measure, a relation to a good object exists, for this also means that the depressive position has been partially worked through. The experience of depression and guilt implies the wish to spare the loved object and to restrict envy.

The defences I have enumerated, and many others, form part of the negative therapeutic reaction because they are a powerful obstacle to the capacity to take in what the analyst has to give. I have referred earlier to some of the forms taken by envy of the analyst. When the patient is able to experience gratitude—and this means that at such times he is less envious—he is in a much better position to benefit by the analysis and to consolidate the gain already achieved. In other words, the more depressive features predominate over schizoid and paranoid features, the better are the prospects of the cure.

The urge to make reparation and the need to help the envied object are also very important means of counteracting envy. Ultimately this involves counteracting destructive impulses by mobilizing feelings of love.

---

[1] Some of my colleagues who analyse schizophrenic cases have told me that the emphasis they are now laying on envy as a spoiling and destructive factor proves of great importance both in understanding and in treating their patients.

II

Since I have referred several times to confusion, it may be useful to summarize some of the important states of confusion as they normally arise at different stages of development and in various connections. I have often pointed out[1] that from the beginning of post-natal life urethral and anal (and even genital) libidinal and aggressive desires are operative—though under the dominance of the oral—and that within a few months the relation to part-objects overlaps with that to whole people.

I have already discussed those factors—in particular strong paranoid-schizoid features and excessive envy—which from the beginning blur the distinction, and impair successful splitting, between the good and bad breast; thus confusion in the infant is reinforced. I believe it essential in analysis to trace all states of confusion in our patients, even the most severe in schizophrenia, to this early inability to distinguish between the good and bad primal object, though the defensive use of confusion against envy and destructive impulses must also be considered.

To enumerate a few consequences of this early difficulty: the premature onset of guilt, the infant's incapacity to experience separately guilt and persecution, and the resulting increase in persecutory anxiety, have already been mentioned above; I have also drawn attention to the importance of the confusion between the parents resulting from an intensification by envy of the combined parent figure. I linked the premature onset of genitality with the flight from orality leading to an increased confusion between oral, anal, and genital trends and phantasies.

[1] Cf. *Psycho-Analysis of Children*, Ch. VIII.

Other factors that make a very early contribution to confusion and perplexed states of mind are projective and introjective identification, because they may temporarily have the effect of blurring the distinction between the self and objects, and between the internal and external world. Such confusion interferes with the recognition of psychic reality, which contributes to the understanding and realistic perception of external reality. Distrust and fear of taking in mental food goes back to the distrust of what the envied and spoiled breast offered. If, primarily, the good food is confused with the bad, later the ability for clear thinking and for developing standards of values is impaired. All these disturbances, which in my view are also bound up with defence against anxiety and guilt, and which are aroused by hate and envy, express themselves in inhibitions in learning and development of the intellect. I am leaving out of account here the various other factors that contribute to such difficulties.

The states of confusion that I have briefly summarized, to which the intense conflict between destructive (hate) and integrating (love) trends contributes, are up to a point normal. It is with growing integration and by working successfully through the depressive position, which includes a greater clarification of internal reality, that the perception of the external world becomes more realistic— a result which is normally well on the way in the second half of the first year and the beginning of the second year.[1] These changes are essentially bound up with a decrease in projective identification, which forms part of paranoid-schizoid mechanisms and anxieties.

----

[1] I have suggested (Cf. *Developments in Psycho-Analysis*) that in the second year of life obsessional mechanisms come to the fore and ego organization occurs under the dominance of anal impulses and phantasies.

CHAPTER SEVEN

I

I SHALL now attempt a brief description of the difficulties that characterize progress during an analysis. To enable the patient to face primary envy and hate only becomes possible after long and painstaking work. Although feelings of competition and envy are familiar to most people, their deepest and earliest implications, experienced in the transference situation, are extremely painful, and therefore difficult, for the patient to accept. The resistance we find in both male and female cases in analysing their Oedipus jealousy and hostility, though very strong, is not as intense as that which we encounter in analysing the envy and hate of the breast. To help a patient to go through these deep conflicts and sufferings is the most effective means of furthering his stability and integration, because it enables him, by means of the transference, to establish more securely his good object and his love for it and to gain some confidence in himself. Needless to say, the analysis of this earliest relation involves the exploration of his later ones, and enables the analyst to understand more fully the patient's adult personality.

In the course of the analysis we have to be prepared to encounter fluctuations between improvement and setbacks. This may show in many ways. For instance, the patient has experienced gratitude and appreciation for the analyst's skill. This very skill, the cause for admiration, soon gives way to envy; envy may be counteracted by pride in having a good analyst. If pride stirs up possessiveness, there may be a revival of infantile greed, which could be expressed in the following terms: I have everything I want; I have the good mother all to myself. Such a greedy and controlling attitude is liable to spoil the relation to the good object and gives rise to guilt, which may soon lead to another defence: for instance, I do not want to injure the analyst-mother, I would rather refrain from accepting her gifts. In this situation the early guilt about rejecting milk and love offered by the mother is revived, because the analyst's help is not accepted. The patient also experiences guilt because he is depriving himself (the good part of his self) of improvement and help, and he reproaches himself for putting too great a burden on the analyst by not sufficiently co-operating; in this way he feels that he is exploiting the analyst. Such attitudes alternate with the persecutory anxiety of being robbed of his defences and emotions, of his thoughts and all his ideals. In states of great anxiety there seems to exist in the patient's mind no other alternative but that he is robbing or being robbed.

Defences, as I have suggested, remain operative even when more insight comes about. Every step nearer to integration, and the anxiety stirred up by this, may lead to early defences appearing with greater strength, and even to new ones. We must also expect that primary envy will come up again and again, and we are therefore confronted with repeated fluctuations in the emotional situation. For instance, when the patient feels despicable, and therefore inferior to the analyst, to whom at that moment he attributes goodness and patience, very soon envy of the analyst reappears. His own unhappiness and the pain and conflicts he goes through are contrasted with what he feels to be the analyst's peace of mind—actually his sanity—and this is a particular cause for envy.

The incapacity of the patient to accept with gratitude an interpretation which in some parts of his mind he recognizes as helpful is one aspect of the negative therapeutic reaction. Under the same heading there are many other difficulties, a few of which I shall now mention. We must be prepared to find that whenever the patient makes progress in integration, that is to say, when the envious, hating and hated part of the personality has come closer together with other parts of the self, intense anxieties might come to the fore, and increase the patient's distrust in his loving impulses. The stifling of love, which I have described as a manic defence during the depressive position, is rooted in the danger threatening from destructive impulses and persecutory anxiety. In an adult, dependence on a loved person revives the helplessness of the infant and is felt to be humiliating. But there is more to it than infantile helplessness: the child can be excessively dependent on the mother, if his anxiety is too great lest his destructive impulses change her into a persecutory or damaged object; and this over-dependence can be revived in the transference situation. The anxiety lest, if one gives way to love, greed should destroy the object, is another cause for stifling loving impulses. There is also the fear that love will lead to too much responsibility and that the object will make too many demands. The unconscious knowledge that hate and destructive impulses are operative may make the patient feel more sincere in not admitting love either to himself or others.

Since no anxiety can arise without the ego using whatever defences it can produce, splitting processes play an important role as methods against experiencing persecutory and depressive anxiety. When we interpret such splitting processes, the patient becomes more conscious of a part of himself of which, because he feels it to be the representative of destructive impulses, he is terrified. With patients in whom early splitting processes (always bound up with schizoid and paranoid features) are less dominant, *repression* of impulses is stronger, and therefore the clinical picture is different. That is to say, we deal then with the more neurotic type of patient, who has succeeded to some extent in overcoming early splitting, and in whom repression has become the main defence against emotional disturbances.

Another difficulty impeding the analysis for long periods is the tenacity with which the patient clings to a strong positive transference; this may to some extent be deceptive because it is based on idealization and covers up the hate and envy which are split off. It is characteristic that oral anxieties are then often avoided and genital elements are in the foreground.

I have tried to show in various connections that destructive impulses, the expression of the death instinct, are first of all felt to be directed against the ego. Confronted with them, even though it has happened gradually, the patient feels exposed to destruction while he is in the process of accepting these impulses as aspects of himself and integrating them. That is to say, the patient at certain times faces several great dangers as a result of integration: his ego may be overwhelmed; the ideal part of his self may be lost when the existence of the split-off, destructive, and hated part of the personality is recognized; the analyst may become hostile and retaliate for the patient's destructive impulses which are no longer repressed, thus also becoming a dangerous super-ego figure; the analyst, in so far as he stands for a good object, is threatened with destruction. The danger to the analyst, which contributes to the strong resistance we meet in attempting to undo splitting and to bring about steps in integration, becomes understandable if we remember that the infant feels his primal object to be the source of goodness and life, and therefore irreplaceable. His anxiety lest he has destroyed it is the cause of major emotional difficulties and enters prominently into the conflicts arising in the depressive position. The feeling of guilt resulting from the realization of destructive envy may lead temporarily to an inhibition of the patient's capacities.

We encounter a very different situation when, as a defence against integration, omnipotent and even megalomanic phantasies increase. This can be a critical stage because the patient may take refuge in reinforcing his hostile attitudes and projections. Thus he thinks himself superior to the analyst, whom he accuses of undervaluing him, and whom in this way he finds some justification for hating. He takes credit for everything so far achieved in the analysis. To go back to the early situation, as an infant, the patient may have had phantasies of being more powerful than his parents, and even that he or she created, as it were, the mother or gave birth to her and possessed the mother's breast. Accordingly it would be the mother who robbed the patient of the breast and not the patient who robbed her. Projection, omnipotence, and persecution are then at their highest. Some of these phantasies are operative whenever feelings of priority in scientific or other work are very strong. There are other factors as well which might stir up the craving for priority such as ambition from various sources, and in particular the feeling of guilt, basically bound up with envy and destruction of the primary object or its later substitutes. For such guilt about robbing the primal object may lead to denial, which takes the form of claiming complete originality and thereby excluding the possibility of having taken or accepted anything from the object.

In the last paragraph I stressed the difficulties arising at certain points in the analysis of patients whose envy is constitutionally strong. However, the analysis of those deep and severe disturbances is in many cases a safeguard against potential danger of psychosis resulting from excessively envious and omnipotent attitudes. But it is essential not to attempt to hurry these steps in integration. For if the realization of the division in his personality were to come suddenly, the patient would have great difficulties in coping with it.[1] The more strongly had the envious and destructive impulses been split off, the more dangerous the patient feels them to be when he becomes conscious of them. In analysis we should make our way slowly and gradually towards the painful insight into the divisions in the patient's self. This means that the destructive sides are again and again split off and regained, until greater integration comes about. As a result, the feeling of responsibility becomes stronger, and guilt and depression are more fully experienced. When this happens, the ego is strengthened, omnipotence of destructive impulses is diminished, together with envy, and the capacity for love and gratitude, stifled in the course of splitting processes, is released. Therefore the split-off aspects gradually become more acceptable and the patient is increasingly able to repress destructive impulses towards loved objects instead of splitting the self. This implies that the projection on the analyst, which turns him into a dangerous and retaliating figure, also diminishes, and that the analyst in turn finds it easier to

---

[1] It might well be that a person who unexpectedly commits a crime or has a psychotic breakdown had suddenly become aware of the split-off dangerous parts of his self. Cases are known of people trying to be arrested in order to prevent themselves from committing a murder.

help the patient towards further integration. That is to say, the negative therapeutic reaction is losing in strength.

It makes great demands both on the analyst and on the patient to analyse splitting processes and the underlying hate and envy both in the positive and negative transference. One consequence of this difficulty is the tendency of some analysts to reinforce the positive and avoid the negative transference, and to attempt to strengthen feelings of love by taking over the role of the good object which the patient had not been able to establish securely in the past. This procedure differs essentially from the technique which, by helping the patient to achieve a better integration of his self, aims at a mitigation of hatred by love. My observations have demonstrated to me that techniques based on reassurance are seldom successful; in particular their results are not lasting. There is indeed an ingrained need for reassurance in everybody, which goes back to the earliest relation to the mother. The infant expects her to attend not only to all his needs, but also craves for signs of her love whenever he experiences anxiety. This longing for reassurance is a vital factor in the analytic situation and we must not underrate its importance in our patients, adults and children alike. We find that though their conscious, and often unconscious, purpose is to be analysed, the patient's strong desire to receive evidence of love and appreciation from the analyst, and thus to be reassured, is never completely given up. Even the patient's co-operation, which allows for an analysis of very deep layers of the mind, of destructive impulses, and of persecutory anxiety, may up to a point be influenced by the urge to satisfy the analyst and to be loved by him. The analyst who is aware of this will analyse the infantile roots of such wishes; otherwise, in identification with his patient, the early need for reassurance may strongly influence his counter-transference and therefore his technique. This identification may also easily tempt the analyst to take the mother's place and give in to the urge immediately to alleviate his child's (the patient's) anxieties.

One of the difficulties of bringing about steps in integration arises when the patient says: 'I can understand what you are telling me but I do not *feel* it.' We are aware that we are in fact referring to a part of the personality which, to all intents and purposes, is not sufficiently accessible either to the patient or to the analyst at that time. Our attempts to help the patient to integrate only carry conviction if we can show him, in the material both present and past, how and why he is again and again splitting off parts of his self. Such evidence is often also provided by a dream preceding the session, and it may be gathered from the whole context of the analytic situation. If an interpretation of splitting is sufficiently supported in the way I described, it might be confirmed in the next session by the patient reporting a bit of a dream or bringing some more material. The cumulative result of such interpretations gradually enables the patient to make some progress in integration and insight.

The anxiety that prevents integration has to be fully understood and interpreted in the transference situation. I have earlier pointed out the threat, both to the self and to the analyst, arising in the patient's mind if split-off parts of the self are regained in the analysis. In dealing with this anxiety one should not underrate the loving impulses when they can be detected in the material. For it is these which in the end enable the patient to mitigate his hate and envy.

However much the patient may at a given moment feel that the interpretation does not strike home, this may often be an expression of resistance. If we have from the beginning of the analysis paid sufficient attention to the ever-repeated attempts to split off destructive parts of the personality, in particular hate and envy, we have in fact, at least in most cases, enabled the patient to make some steps towards integration. It is only after painstaking, careful, and consistent work on the part of the analyst that we can expect a more stable integration in the patient.

I shall now illustrate this phase in the analysis by two dreams.

The second male patient I referred to, at a later stage of his analysis, when greater integration and improvement in various ways had occurred, reported the following dream, which shows the fluctuations in the process of integration caused by the pain of depressive feelings. He was in an upstairs flat and 'X', a friend of a friend of his, was calling him from the street suggesting a walk together. The patient did not join 'X', because a black dog in the flat might get out and be run over. He stroked the dog. When he looked out of the window, he found that 'X' had 'receded'.

Some of the associations brought the flat into connection with mine and the black dog with my black cat, which he described as 'she'. The patient never liked 'X', who was an old fellow-student of his. He described him as suave and insincere; 'X' also often borrowed money (though he returned it later) and did so in a manner which suggested that he had every right to ask for such favours. 'X' turned out, however, to be very good in his profession.

The patient recognized that 'a friend of his friend' was one aspect of himself. The gist of my interpretations was that he had come closer to realizing an unpleasant and frightening part of his personality; the danger to the dog-cat—the analyst—was that she would be run over (that is to say, injured) by 'X'. When 'X' had been asking him to join him for a walk, this symbolized a step towards integration.

At this stage a hopeful element entered into the dream by the association that 'X', in spite of his faults, had turned out to be good in his profession. It is also characteristic of progress that the side of himself to which he came closer in this dream was not so destructive and envious as in previous material.

The patient's concern with the safety of the dog-cat expressed the wish to protect the analyst against his own hostile and greedy tendencies, represented by 'X', and led to a temporary widening of the split that had already partly been healed. When, however, 'X', the rejected part of himself, 'receded', this showed that he had not altogether gone and that the process of integration was only temporarily disturbed. The mood of the patient at that time was characterized by depression; guilt towards the analyst and the wish to preserve her were prominent. In this context, the fear of integration was caused by the feeling that the analyst must be protected from the patient's repressed greedy and dangerous impulses. I had no doubt that he was still splitting off a part of his personality, but the *repression* of greedy and destructive impulses had become more noticeable. The interpretation, therefore, had to deal both with splitting and with repression.

The first man patient also brought at a later stage of his analysis a dream that showed rather more advanced steps in integration. He dreamed that he had a delinquent brother who committed a serious crime. He had been received in a house and had killed the inhabitants and robbed them. The patient was deeply disturbed by this but felt that he must be loyal to his brother and save him. They fled together and found themselves in a boat. Here the patient associated *Les Misérables* by Victor Hugo, and mentioned Javert who had persecuted an innocent person all his life and even followed him right into the sewers of Paris where he was hiding. But Javert ended by committing suicide because he had recognized that he had spent his whole life in the wrong way.

The patient then went on with his account of the dream. He and his brother were arrested by a policeman who looked kindly at him, and so the patient hoped he would not be executed after all; he seemed to leave his brother to his fate.

The patient realized at once that the delinquent brother was part of himself. He had recently used the expression 'delinquent' referring to very minor matters in his own conduct. We shall also remember here that in a previous dream he had referred to a delinquent boy with whom he could not deal.

The step in integration to which I am referring was shown by the patient taking the responsibility for the delinquent brother and by being with him in 'the same boat'. I interpreted the crime of murdering and robbing the people who had kindly received him as his phantasied attacks on the analyst, and referred to his often-expressed anxiety lest his greedy wish to get as much out of me as possible would harm me. I linked this with the early guilt in relation to his mother. The kindly policeman stood for the analyst who would not judge him harshly and would help him to get rid of the bad part of himself. I pointed out, moreover, that in the process of integration the use of splitting—both of the self and of the object—had reappeared. This was shown by the analyst figuring in a double role: as the kindly policeman and the persecutory Javert, who in the end took his own life, and on whom the patient's 'badness' was also projected. Although the patient had understood his responsibility for the 'delinquent' part of his personality, he was still splitting his self. For he was represented by the 'innocent' man, whereas the sewers into which he was pursued meant the depths of his anal and oral destructiveness.

The recurrence of splitting was caused not only by persecutory but also by depressive anxiety, for the patient felt
that he could not confront the analyst (when she appeared
in a kindly role) with the bad part of himself without harming her. This was one of the reasons why he resorted to
uniting with the policeman against the bad part of himself,
which at that moment he wished to annihilate.

II

Freud early accepted that some individual variations in
development are due to constitutional factors: for instance, he expressed in 'Character and Anal Erotism'
(1908) the view that strong anal erotism is in many people
constitutional.[1] Abraham discovered an innate element in
the strength of oral impulses, which he connected with
the aetiology of manic-depressive illness. He said that ' . . .
what really is constitutional and inherited is an over-accen-
tuation of oral erotism in the same way that in certain
families anal erotism seems to be a preponderant factor
from the very beginning.'[2]

I have previously suggested that greed, hate, and persecutory anxieties in relation to the primal object, the
mother's breast, have an innate basis. In this book I have
added that envy, as a powerful expression of oral- and anal-
sadistic impulses, is also constitutional. The variations in
the intensity of these constitutional factors are in my view
linked with the preponderance of the one or other instinct
in the fusion of the life and death instincts postulated by

---

[1] 'From these indications we infer that the erotogenic significance of the
anal zone is intensified in the innate sexual constitution of these persons.'

[2] 'A Short History of the Development of the Libido' (1924).

Freud. I believe there is a connection between this pre-ponderance of the one or other instinct and the strength or weakness of the ego. I have often referred to the strength of the ego in relation to the anxieties it has to cope with as a constitutional factor. Difficulties in bearing anxiety, tension, and frustration are an expression of an ego which, from the beginning of post-natal life, is weak in proportion to the intense destructive impulses and persecutory feelings it experiences. These strong anxieties imposed on a weak ego lead to an excessive use of defences such as denial, splitting, and omnipotence, which to some extent are always characteristic of earliest development. In keeping with my thesis, I would add that a constitutionally strong ego does not easily become a prey to envy and is more capable of effecting the splitting between good and bad which I assume to be a precondition for establishing the good object. The ego is then less liable to those splitting processes which lead to fragmentation and are part of marked paranoid-schizoid features.

Another factor that influences development from the beginning is the variety of external experiences through which the infant goes. This in some measure explains the development of his early anxieties, which would be particularly great in a baby who had a difficult birth and unsatisfactory feeding. My accumulated observations, however, have convinced me that the impact of these external experiences is in proportion to the constitutional strength of the innate destructive impulses and the ensuing paranoid anxieties. Many infants have not had very unfavourable experiences and yet suffer from serious difficulties in feeding and sleeping, and we can see in them every sign of great anxiety for which external circumstances do not account sufficiently.

It is also well known that some infants are exposed to

great deprivations and unfavourable circumstances, and yet do not develop excessive anxieties, which would suggest that their paranoid and envious traits are not predominant; this is often confirmed by their later history.

I have had many opportunities in my analytic work to trace the origin of character formation to variations in innate factors. There is much more to be learnt about pre-natal influences; but even greater knowledge about them would not detract from the importance of inborn elements in determining the strength of the ego and of instinctual drives.

The existence of the innate factors referred to above points to the limitations of psycho-analytic therapy. While I fully realize this, my experience has taught me that never-theless we are able in a number of cases to produce funda-mental and positive changes, even where the constitutional basis was unfavourable.

CONCLUSION

For many years the envy of the feeding breast as a factor which adds intensity to the attacks on the primal object has been part of my analyses. It is, however, only more recently that I have laid particular emphasis on the spoiling and destructive quality of envy in so far as it interferes with the building up of a secure relation to the good external and internal object, undermines the sense of gratitude, and in many ways blurs the distinction between good and bad.

In all the cases I have described, the relation to the analyst as an internal object was of fundamental importance. This I found to be true generally. When anxiety about envy and its consequences reaches a climax, the patient in varying degrees feels persecuted by the analyst as an internal grudging and envious object, disturbing his work, life, and activities. When this occurs, the good object is felt to be lost, and with it inner security. My observations have shown me that when, at any stage in life, the relation to the good object is seriously disturbed—a disturbance in which envy plays a prominent role—not only are inner security and peace interfered with but character deterioration sets in. The prevalence of internal persecutory objects reinforces destructive impulses; whereas, if the good object is well established, the identification with it strengthens the capacity for love, constructive impulses, and gratitude. This is in keeping with the hypothesis

I put forward at the beginning of this book: if the good object is deeply rooted, temporary disturbances may be withstood and the foundation of mental health, of character formation, and of successful ego development is laid.

I have described in other connections the importance of the earliest internalized persecutory object—the retaliating, devouring, and poisonous breast. I would now assume that the projection of the infant's envy lends a particular complexion to his anxiety about the primal and later internal persecution. The 'envious super-ego' is felt to disturb or annihilate all attempts at reparation and creativeness. It is also felt to make constant and exorbitant demands on the individual's gratitude. For to persecution are added the guilt feelings that the persecutory internal objects are the result of the individual's own envious and destructive impulses which have primarily spoilt the good object. The need for punishment, which finds satisfaction by the increased devaluation of the self, leads to a vicious circle.

As we all know, the ultimate aim of psycho-analysis is the integration of the patient's personality. Freud's conclusion that where Id was, Ego shall be, is a pointer in that direction. Splitting processes arise in the earliest stages of development. If they are excessive, they form an integral part of severe paranoid and schizoid features which may be the basis of schizophrenia. In normal development, these schizoid and paranoid trends (the paranoid-schizoid position) are, to a large extent, overcome during the period which is characterized by the depressive position, and integration develops successfully. The important steps towards integration introduced during that stage prepare the capacity of the ego for repression, which I believe increasingly operates in the second year of life.

In *Developments in Psycho-Analysis*[1] I suggested that the young child is able to deal with emotional difficulties by repression if splitting processes in the early stages have not been too powerful, and therefore a consolidation of the conscious and unconscious parts of the mind has come about. In the earliest stages splitting and other defence mechanisms are always paramount. Already, in *Inhibition, Symptoms and Anxiety*, Freud had suggested that there may be methods of defence earlier than repression. In the present book I have not dealt with the vital significance of repression for normal development, because the effect of primary envy and its close connection with splitting processes have been my main subject matter.

As regards technique, I have attempted to show that by analysing over and over again the anxieties and defences bound up with envy and destructive impulses, progress in integration can be achieved. I have always been convinced of the importance of Freud's finding that 'working-through' is one of the main tasks of the analytic procedure, and my experience in dealing with splitting processes and tracing them back to their origin had made this conviction even stronger. The deeper and more complex the difficulties we are analysing, the greater is the resistance we are likely to encounter, and this has a bearing on the necessity to give adequate scope to 'working-through'.

This necessity arises particularly with regard to envy of the primary object. Patients might recognize their envy, jealousy, and competitive attitudes towards other people, even the wish to harm their faculties, but only the analyst's perseverance in analysing these hostile feelings in the transference, and thereby enabling the patient to re-experience them in his earliest relation, can lead to the splitting within the self being diminished.

[1] Chapter VI.

My experience has shown me that when the analysis of these fundamental impulses, phantasies, and emotions fails, this is partly because the pain and depressive anxiety made manifest, in some people outweigh the desire for truth and, ultimately, the desire to be helped. I believe that a patient's co-operation has to be based on a strong determination to discover the truth about himself if he is to accept and assimilate the analyst's interpretations relating to these early layers of the mind. For these interpretations, if deep enough, mobilize a part of the self that is felt as an enemy to the ego as well as to the loved object, and has, therefore, been split off and annihilated. I have found that the anxieties aroused by interpretations of hate and envy toward the primal object, and the feeling of persecution by the analyst whose work stirs up those emotions, are more painful than any other material we interpret.

These difficulties apply particularly to patients with strong paranoid anxieties and schizoid mechanisms, for they are less able to experience, side by side with the persecutory anxiety stirred up by interpretations, a positive transference and trust in the analyst—ultimately they are less capable of maintaining feelings of love. At the present stage of our knowledge, I am inclined to the view that these are the patients, not necessarily of a manifest psychotic type, with whom success is limited, or may not be achieved.

When the analysis can be carried to these depths, envy and the fear of envy diminish, leading to a greater trust in constructive and reparative forces, actually in the capacity for love. The result is also greater tolerance towards one's own limitations, as well as improved object relations and a clearer perception of internal and external reality.

The insight gained in the process of integration makes it possible, in the course of the analysis, for the patient to recognize that there are potentially dangerous parts of his self. But when love can be sufficiently brought together with the split-off hate and envy, these emotions become bearable and diminish, because they are mitigated by love. The various anxiety contents mentioned earlier are also lessened, such as the danger of being overwhelmed by a split-off, destructive part of the self. This danger seems all the greater because, as a consequence of excessive early omnipotence, the harm done in phantasy appears irrevocable. The anxiety lest hostile feelings destroy the loved objects diminishes when these feelings become better known and are integrated in the personality. The pain the patient experiences during the analysis is also gradually lessened by improvements bound up with progress in integration, such as regaining some initiative, becoming able to make decisions he was previously unable to reach and, in general, using his gifts more freely. This is linked up with a lessening inhibition of his capacity to make reparation. His power of enjoyment increases in many ways, and hope reappears, though it may still alternate with depression. I have found that creativeness grows in proportion to being able to establish the good object more securely, which in successful cases is the result of the analysis of envy and destructiveness.

Similarly, as in infancy, repeated happy experiences of being fed and loved are instrumental in establishing securely the good object, so during an analysis repeated experiences of the effectiveness and truth of the interpretations given lead to the analyst—and retrospectively the primal object —being built up as good figures.

All these changes amount to an enrichment of the personality. Together with hate, envy, and destructiveness, other important parts of the self which had been lost are regained in the course of the analysis. There is also considerable relief in feeling more of a whole person, in gain-ing control over one's own self, and in a deeper sense of security in relation to the world in general. In 'Some Schizoid Mechanisms' I have suggested that the sufferings of the schizophrenic, due to his feelings of being split in bits, are most intense. These sufferings are underrated because his anxieties appear in a different form from those of the neurotic. Even when we are not dealing with psychotics, but are analysing people whose integration had been disturbed and who feel uncertain both about themselves and others, similar anxieties are experienced and are relieved when fuller integration is achieved. Complete and permanent integration is in my view never possible. For under strain from external or internal sources, even well integrated people may be driven to stronger splitting processes, even though this may be a passing phase.

In a paper, 'On Identification',[1] I suggested how important it is for the development of mental health and personality that in the early splitting processes fragmentation should not dominate. I wrote there: 'The feeling of containing an unharmed nipple and breast—although co-existing with phantasies of a breast devoured and therefore in bits—has the effect that splitting and projecting are not *predominantly* related to fragmented parts of the personality but to more coherent parts of the self. This implies that the ego is not exposed to a fatal weakening by dispersal and for this reason is more capable of repeatedly undoing splitting and achieving integration and synthesis in its relation to objects.'[2]

I believe this capacity to regain the split-off parts of the personality to be a precondition for normal development. This implies that splitting is to some extent overcome

[1] *New Directions in Psycho-Analysis.*

[2] Page 313.

during the depressive position and that repression of impulses and phantasies gradually takes its place.

Character analysis has always been an important and very difficult part of analytic therapy.[1] It is, I believe, through tracing back certain aspects of character formation to the early processes I have described that we can, in a number of cases, effect far-reaching changes in character and personality.

We can consider from another angle the aspects of technique which I have tried to convey in this book. From the beginning, all emotions attach themselves to the first object. If destructive impulses, envy, and paranoid anxiety are excessive, the infant grossly distorts and magnifies every frustration from outer sources, and the mother's breast turns externally and internally predominantly into a persecutory object. Then even actual gratifications cannot sufficiently counteract persecutory anxiety. In taking the analysis back to earliest infancy, we enable the patient to revive fundamental situations—a revival which I have often spoken of as 'memories in feeling'. In the course of this revival, it becomes possible for the patient to develop a different attitude to his early frustrations. There is no doubt that if the infant was actually exposed to very unfavourable conditions, the retrospective establishing of a good object cannot undo bad early experiences. However, the introjection of the analyst as a good object, if not based on idealization has, to some extent, the effect of providing an internal good object where it has been largely lacking. Also,

[1] The most fundamental contributions to this topic have been made by Freud, Jones, and Abraham. Cf. for instance, Freud 'Character and Anal Erotism' (1908), Jones 'Hate and Anal-Erotism in the Obsessional Neuroses' (1913) and 'Anal-Erotic Character Traits' (1918), and Abraham 'Contributions to the Theory of the Anal Character' (1921), 'The Influence of Oral Erotism on Character Formation' (1924), and 'Character Formation on the Genital Level of Libido Development' (1925).

the weakening of projections, and therefore the achieving of greater tolerance, bound up with less resentment, make it possible for the patient to find some features and to revive pleasant memories of the past, even when the early situation was very unfavourable. The means by which this is achieved is the analysis of the negative and positive transference which takes us back to earliest object relations. All this becomes possible because the integration resulting from the analysis has strengthened the ego, which was weak at the beginning of life. It is on these lines that the psychoanalysis of psychotics may also succeed. The more integrated ego becomes capable of experiencing guilt and feelings of responsibility, which it was unable to face in infancy; object synthesis, and therefore a mitigation of hate by love, come about, and greed and envy, which are corollaries of destructive impulses, lose in power.

To express it in another way, persecutory anxiety and schizoid mechanisms are diminished, and the patient can work through the depressive position. When his initial inability to establish a good object is, to some extent, overcome, envy is diminished and his capacity for enjoyment and gratitude increases step by step. These changes extend to many aspects of the patient's personality and range from earliest emotional life to adult experiences and relations. In the analysis of the effects of early disturbances on the whole development, lies, I believe, our greatest hope of helping our patients.

BIBLIOGRAPHY

ABRAHAM, K. (1921) 'Contribution to the Theory of the Anal Character.'

(1924) 'The Influence of Oral Erotism on Character Formation.'

(1924) 'A Short History of the Development of the Libido, Viewed in the Light of Mental Disorders.'

(1925) 'Character Formation on the Genital Level of Libido Development.'

All the above papers are published in *Selected Papers on Psycho-Analysis*, London, Hogarth Press, 1927.

BION, W. R. (1954) 'Notes on the Theory of Schizophrenia.' *Int. J. Psycho-Anal.*, Vol. xxxv, Part II.

(1955) 'Differentiation of the Psychotic from the Non-Psychotic Personalities.' Paper delivered at the 19th International Psycho-Analytical Congress.

FREUD, S. (1905) *Three Essays on the Theory of Sexuality*, London, Hogarth Press, 1949.

(1908) 'Character and Anal Erotism.' *Collected Papers*, Vol. II, London, Hogarth Press, 1924.

(1915) 'Some Character-Types Met with in Psycho-Analytic Work.' *Collected Papers*, Vol. IV, London, Hogarth Press, 1925.

(1923) *The Ego and the Id*, London, Hogarth Press, 1927.

(1926) *Inhibitions, Symptoms and Anxiety*, London, Hogarth Press, 1936.

(1937) 'Analysis Terminable and Interminable.' *Collected Papers*, Vol. V, London, Hogarth Press, 1950.

(1938) 'Construction in Analysis.' *Collected Papers*, Vol. V, London, Hogarth Press, 1950.

JONES, E. (1913) 'Hate and Anal Erotism in the Obsessional Neurosis.' *Int. Z. (ärztl.) Psychoan.*, Jahrgang I, Heft 5. (*Papers on Psycho-Analysis*, London, Ballière, Tindall & Cox, 1918.)

(1918) 'Anal-Erotic Character Traits.' *Papers on Psycho-Analysis*, 1948 edition, London, Ballière, Tindall & Cox.

KLEIN, M. (1928) 'Early Stages of the Oedipus Conflict.' *Contributions to Psycho-Analysis, 1921-1945*, London, Hogarth Press, 1948.

(1930) 'The Importance of Symbol-Formation in the Development of the Ego.' *Contributions to Psycho-Analysis*, London, Hogarth Press, 1948.

(1932) *The Psycho-Analysis of Children*, London, Hogarth Press, 1932.

(1935) 'A Contribution to the Psychogenesis of Manic-Depressive States.' *Contributions to Psycho-Analysis*, London, Hogarth Press, 1948.

(1940) 'Mourning and its Relation to Manic-Depressive States.' *Contributions to Psycho-Analysis*, London, Hogarth Press, 1948.

(1945) 'The Oedipus Complex in the Light of Early Anxieties.' *Contributions to Psycho-Analysis*, London, Hogarth Press, 1948.

(1946) 'Notes on Some Schizoid Mechanisms.' *Developments in Psycho-Analysis*, London, Hogarth Press, 1952.

(1948) *Contributions to Psycho-Analysis*, London, Hogarth Press.

(1955) 'On Identification.' *New Directions in Psycho-Analysis*, London, Tavistock Publications, 1955.

KLEIN, M., HEIMANN, P., ISAACS, S., and RIVIERE, J. (1951) *Developments in Psycho-Analysis*, London, Hogarth Press, 1952.

RIVIERE, J. (1932) 'Jealousy as a Mechanism of Defence.' *Int. J. Psycho-Anal.*, Vol. XIII.

(1936) 'A Contribution to the Analysis of the Negative Therapeutic Reaction.' *Int. J. Psycho-Anal.*, Vol. XVII.

ROSENFELD, H. (1947) 'Analysis of a Schizophrenic State with Depersonalization.' *Int. J. Psycho-Anal.*, Vol. XXVIII.

(1950) 'A Note on the Psychopathology of Confusional States in Chronic Schizophrenias.' *Int. J. Psycho-Anal.*, Vol. XXXI.

(1955) 'The Investigation of the Need of Neurotic and Psychotic Patients to Act Out during Analysis.' Paper read to the 19th International Psycho-Analytical Congress.

WINNICOTT, D. W. (1953) 'Psychoses and Child Care.' *Collected Papers: through Paediatrics to Psycho-Analysis.* London, Tavistock Publications, 1957 (in press).

INDEX

Abraham, ix, x, 1, 15, 36, 81, 90n, 92
Acting-out, 66, 66n
Ambition, 35, 42, 58–60, 74
Anal erotism, 81, 90n
Anal impulses, 30, 68, 69n
Anxiety (*see also* Depressive anxiety, Fear, Persecutory anxiety)
  defences against, *see* Defences
  as inevitable, 14–15
  insight leading to, 71–81, 87–8
  and need for reassurance, 4, 76
  tolerance of, 61, 82

Bion, W., 30n, 92
Birth
  difficulties at, 4, 82
  and persecutory anxiety, 4, 82
Breast (*see also* Mother, Mother's body, Object)
  attacked, spoiled, 6n, 7, 10n, 10–11, 15, 17–18, 23, 29, 36, 58ff., 62–3, 65, 73–4, 84, 89
  bad, hated, 4, 5, 10, 13, 16, 23–4, 24–5, 62–3, 70
  creative, 5–6, 7, 39, 62–3
  enjoyed, 3, 15–16, 17–21, 23, 42, 45–6
  envied, 6, 10–11, 18, 19–20, 29, 31, 36ff., 43ff., 52, 53ff., 58ff., 70, 84

  frustrating, 4, 6, 10, 11, 13–14, 18n, 44–5, 49
  good, loved, 3–4, 5–6, 17, 17–21, 24, 25–6, 39
  idealized, 24ff.
  'illusory', 19n
  inexhaustible, 4, 5–6, 10, 11, 14
  internalized, 3, 4, 5, 6, 7, 17, 18–19, 23ff., 65, 89, 90
  lost and regained, 5, 7, 15–16, 32, 45–6, 62, 63, 74
  penis equated with, 35ff.
  persecuting, 25, 85, 90
  as source of goodness, 3, 5–6, 10, 39, 74

Castration, 35
Chaucer, 20, 41n
Combined parents, 33–4, 68
Confusion
  of good and bad object, 12–13, 23–4, 26, 62, 68–9, 84
  of impulses, 29–30, 68
  of internal and external, 69
  between parents, 33–4, 68
  of self and non-self, 25, 69
Corinthians, 40
Creativeness
  of breast (mother), 5–6, 7, 10, 39–40
  capacity for, 41, 87–8

envied and spoilt, 7, 10–12, 40–1,
55ff., 85
frustration leading to, 15
Criticism
constructive, 41
destructive, 12, 26–7, 40–1, 55ff.,
63–4

Death instinct (see also Destructive
impulses, Life instinct), 4, 22,
61, 73
Defences (see also Denial, Idealization, Manic defence, Omnipotence, Projection, Reassurance, Repression, Splitting),
12–13, 14, 16, 19, 20–1, 22–4,
24–7, 28–31, 34–5, 36–9,
61ff., 70ff., 82, 85ff.
Denial, 29, 31, 54–5, 59, 62, 66,
72, 73, 74, 82
Depression, 28n, 31, 47, 50–5,
58ff., 64, 67, 75, 78, 88
Depressive anxiety, 27, 28, 30, 55,
57, 58ff., 62–3, 64–5, 66, 72,
75, 80–1, 87–8
Depressive position, 23, 25, 28,
30–1, 32–3, 61, 62–3, 65, 67,
69, 72, 85, 89–91
Deprivation (see also Frustration),
4–5, 11, 13–14, 16n, 71, 82,
90
Destructive impulses (see also Death
instinct)
towards analyst, 12, 43–60, 64
anxiety about (see Depressive anxiety)
towards breast (mother), 6n, 7, 9,
10–11, 15, 17–18, 29, 36,
47–8, 53ff., 58ff., 62

defences against (see Defences)
fear of, 4–5, 73, 75, 84, 87–8
as innate, 5, 81, 82
Disintegration (see Splitting)
Dreams, 44ff., 48ff., 51ff., 53ff.,
56ff., 58–9, 59–60, 77, 78ff.

Early emotional life
and adult personality, 3ff., 17, 18,
20, 24, 42, 70, 76, 90–1
reconstructed in analysis, 1–3, 13,
45–6, 70ff., 86ff., 90
Ego
-annihilation, 4–5, 22, 61, 73
building up of, 3–6, 15, 17, 18–
19, 22–4, 28, 84–5
constitutional strength of, 61,
81–2
-defences (see Defences)
-disintegration (see Splitting)
-integration, 22–7, 28, 31, 32,
43–60, 66, 69, 70–91
synthesizing function of, 24, 25,
31, 32, 52, 89, 91
Enjoyment
capacity for, 41–2, 45–6, 57–8,
88, 91
envy of, 11, 41, 45
envy spoiling, 13, 16, 18, 19–20,
29, 38, 41, 44, 65
genital, 18, 29–30, 38
in old age, 41–2
Envy
ambition leading to, 35, 58–60,
74
anal origin of, ix, 6n, 7, 15, 48–
51, 58–9, 81
of analyst, 11–13, 34–5, 43–60,
64, 67, 70ff., 86

of breast, 6, 10, 11, 15, 18, 19–
20, 29, 31, 33, 35, 36–8, 38–9,
43ff., 70, 71, 84
as constitutional, ix, 81
of contentment, 11, 41, 45
of creativeness, 7, 11–12, 40,
53ff., 58ff.
criticism expressing, 11–12, 27,
40, 41n, 63–4
defences against, 12–13, 16, 26,
29–30, 34–5, 36, 37, 61–7,
70ff., 85, 86
definition of, 6–9
destructiveness of, ix, 6, 7, 8–9,
10–12, 15–16, 18, 20, 34, 35,
36, 39, 40–1, 47–60, 62, 63–4,
65, 66, 74, 78–9, 79–81, 84–5,
86, 88
enjoyment spoilt by (see Enjoyment)
of father, 35, 53ff.
gratitude destroyed by (see Gratitude)
and greed, 7, 8, 16, 26, 65, 71
guilt about, 12, 28ff., 34, 50, 52,
64–5, 67, 71, 74, 75, 85
and jealousy, 6ff., 10, 31–9
of mother's role, 6n, 10, 34,
36ff., 40
oral origin of, ix–x, 6, 9, 10–11,
34, 68, 81
of penis, 35ff.
and pride, 71
in psychosis, 22ff., 62, 67, 68,
74–5
of sanity, 41, 72
External reality
adaptation to, 4, 15, 28n, 32, 69,
87, 89, 90–1
confused with internal, 69

importance of, 4–5, 13n, 14–15,
16n, 17–19, 31, 33, 82–3, 88,
90

Father (see also Penis)
combined with mother, 33–4, 57,
68
envy and jealousy of, 32ff., 53ff.
idealized, 37
turning to, 32, 36ff., 57, 63
'Faerie Queene', 40
Fear (see also Anxiety)
of annihilation, 22, 39, 61, 73
greed caused by, 8
of helplessness, 72
in jealousy, 7–8, 32–3
of madness, 51–3
Feeding
disturbance in, 4, 11, 13, 14–15,
16n, 43–6, 57–8, 82
enjoyment in, 15–16, 18–21, 23,
29, 42, 45–6
-situation, 3–6, 11, 13–14, 14–
15, 16n, 82
Feminine position, 10, 38–9, 53ff.
Freud, x, 1–3, 13n, 18, 22, 35, 36,
52n, 81–2, 85, 86, 90n, 92
Frigidity, 38
Frustration (see also Deprivation)
by breast (mother), 4, 6, 11, 13–
14, 16n, 43–6, 90
and sublimation, 15
tolerance of, 90–1

Generosity, ix, 6, 19
Genital impulses, 18, 29–30, 35–9,
68, 73, 81n, 90n
Goethe, 42

Gratitude
    in analysis, 11–12, 45–6, 50, 58,
        60, 67, 71, 72
    capacity for, 6, 16, 17ff., 41, 46,
        58, 72, 75, 84, 91
    envy destroying, ix, 6, 16, 20, 46,
        50, 58, 84
    guilt leading to, 20, 85
    and reparation, 19
    and sublimation, 19
Greed
    in analysis, 16, 43ff., 79
    anxiety about, 16, 27, 72, 79
    definition of, 7–8
    envy interacting with, 7–8, 16,
        65, 71
    identification based on, 16, 26
    in introjection, 7, 18, 23, 65
Guilt
    depressive (see Depressive an-
        xiety)
    gratitude based on, 20, 85
    as persecutory, 28–9, 58, 68, 85
    premature, 28–9, 30, 68
    and reparation, 28, 58, 85

Hate (see also Love, Splitting)
    indifference concealing, 66
    love mitigating, 25, 31, 67, 76,
        77, 91
    Oedipal, 32–9
Homosexuality, 36, 37, 38, 57

Idealization, 4, 24–7, 37, 50, 62, 63,
        64, 73, 90
Identification
    with good object, 25–6, 41, 84
    indiscriminate, 16, 25, 26, 27
    with injured object, 57, 62

introjective (see Introjective iden-
        tification)
    projective (see Projective identifi-
        cation)
    and sublimation, 34
Innate factors, ix, 5, 17, 61, 81–3
Insight
    anxiety through, 71ff., 87–8
    depression through, 50–1, 53ff.,
        59–60
    integration through, 43–60, 71–
        81, 85ff.
Integration
    through analysis, 43–60, 70–81,
        85–91
    and depressive anxiety, 28, 31
    and capacity to love, 22–3, 24,
        25–6, 69
    resistance to, 66, 70–81
Internal reality, 28n, 30, 69
Introjection, 3, 5–6, 7, 16–17, 18–
        19, 23ff., 52–3, 65, 84–5, 89,
        90, 91
Introjective identification, 69

Jaques, E., 7n
Jealousy
    definition of, 7–9
    and envy, 7–9, 10n
    Oedipal, 31ff., 49, 70
Jones, E., 90n, 93

Life instinct (see also Death instinct)
    and capacity for love, 26, 39
    in struggle with death instinct,
        22–4
Love (see also Hate, Splitting)
    belief in own, 6, 16, 19, 20, 25–7,
        70, 72, 88–9

capacity for, 6, 17–21, 23, 24, 25–7, 41–2, 75, 84
hate mitigated by, 25, 31, 67, 76, 77, 91
idealization versus, 24–7
rejection of, 13, 26, 71–2
stifling of, 66, 72

Manic defence (see also Defences, Denial, Idealization, Omnipotence, Splitting), 31, 47–51, 71, 74
Manic depression, x, 15, 27n, 81
Masturbation, 30
Mental illness (see also Manic depression, Schizophrenia), x, 23–4, 30n, 33–4, 61, 62, 75, 89, 91
Milton, 40
Mother (see also Breast, Object)
  boy's relation to, 10, 34, 38–9, 53ff., 58ff.
  creativeness of, 5–6, 7, 10, 40, 58ff.
  earliest relation to, 3ff., 10ff., 14ff., 17ff., 23ff., 31ff., 39, 43ff., 76
  father combined with, 33–4, 68
  girl's relation to, 6n, 10, 34, 35ff.
  identification with, 34, 39, 62
  loss of, 7, 32–3, 62, 63
  as omnipotent, 4–5, 14
  over-anxious, 14–15
  over-dependence on, 72
  with penis, 32, 33, 35n, 37
  turning away from, 36ff., 57, 63, 71
Mothering, 4, 13n, 17

Mother's body (see also Breast)
  attacks on, 6n, 7, 9, 10–11, 40, 47ff., 51ff., 53ff.
  phantasies about, 6n, 32, 33, 35n
Mourning, 27n, 32

Object (see also Breast, Father, Mother, Psycho-analyst)
  attacked, spoilt, 10–13, 15–16, 20, 29, 30, 35, 47ff., 52, 53ff., 58ff., 62, 63–4, 65, 67, 84–5
  doubts about, 11–13, 16, 26–7, 31, 69
  establishing of, 3ff., 13, 17ff., 24, 25, 26–7, 29, 31, 42, 65, 88, 91
  good and bad confused, 12–13, 23–4, 26, 62, 68–9, 84
  good and bad distinguished, 23–4, 82
  idealized (see Idealization)
  lost and regained, 5, 6–7, 15–16, 17, 20, 27, 32, 43–6, 63, 84–5
  loved and loving, 4–6, 17ff., 25, 26, 39, 42, 65, 84, 87, 88
  omnipotently controlled, 18, 65, 71, 74
  persecuting, 11, 24ff., 28–9, 40, 54–5, 62, 65, 69, 84–5, 90
  preserving of, 23, 24, 31, 60, 63, 65, 67, 89
  splitting of (see Splitting)
  synthesized, 24, 28n, 31, 32, 89, 91
Object relations
  insecure, 6, 13–14, 16, 19–21, 25ff., 32, 62ff., 84, 91
  Oedipal, 28n, 32ff.

promiscuous, 30, 38, 63
secure, 3, 5–6, 17, 18ff., 25ff., 31,
    32, 42, 65, 67, 70, 85, 87, 88
widening of, 32, 63
Obsessional mechanisms, 69n
Oedipus complex, 1, 6n, 28n, 32ff.,
    49, 57, 70
Omnipotence, 18, 20, 29, 47, 62,
    65, 71, 74, 75, 82, 88
Oral impulses
    constitutional factor in, ix–x, 81
    and genitality, 18, 29–30, 34,
    35n, 36ff., 68, 73
Oral sadism, ix, x, 6n, 7, 9, 15, 81
Othello, 8

Paradise Lost, 40
Paranoid mechanisms, 10, 13, 23,
    26–7, 28–9, 33, 52, 67, 68, 69,
    73, 83, 85, 87
Paranoid-schizoid position, 23, 24,
    28, 85
Penis (*see also* Father)
    breast equated with, 36
    child equated with, 35n
    envy of, 35ff.
    idealization of, 37
    mother containing, 32, 33ff.
    turning to, 36ff.
Persecutory anxiety, 4–5, 11, 14,
    16, 19, 20, 22–7, 28–9, 33,
    53ff., 58, 59, 61ff., 68–9, 71ff.,
    81, 82, 84–5, 87, 90–1
Phantasies
    about breast, 5–6, 10, 32, 33, 89
    of combined parents, 33–4, 68
    about mother's body, 6n, 32, 33,
    35n
    Oedipal, 32ff.
    pre-verbal, 5n

Promiscuity, 30, 38, 63
Projection, 7, 25, 27, 29, 31, 40,
    45, 53, 57, 74, 75, 84, 85, 91
Projective identification, 6n, 7, 25,
    45, 69
Psycho-analysis
    difficulties in, 70ff.
    of dreams, 43–60, 78–81
    material from, 43–60, 64, 78–81
    negative therapeutic reaction in,
    11–13, 14, 64, 67, 70ff.
    of psychotics, 67n, 91
    reassurance in, 76
    reconstruction in, 1–3, 5–6, 13,
    43–60, 70ff., 84, 86, 88, 90
    of splitting, 12, 14, 43–60, 70ff.,
    85, 86–91
Psycho-analyst (*see also* Transference)
    concern for, 46, 50–1, 53–7, 59–
    60, 71, 73–4, 75, 77, 79, 80–1
    criticized and devalued, 11–13,
    34–5, 43–6, 47–51, 56–7, 58–
    60, 63–4, 74
    doubts about, 11–13, 16, 46, 49
    envy and jealousy of, 11–13, 34–5,
    43–60, 64, 67, 70ff., 86
    gratitude towards, 11–13, 45–6,
    50, 58, 60, 67, 71, 72
    greed towards, 16, 43ff., 79
    guilt towards, 12, 29, 50, 59–60,
    71, 74, 79, 80
    idealization of, 73
    internalized, 84, 88, 90
    over-dependence on, 72, 76
    persecution by, 29, 43ff., 54–5,
    59, 71, 73, 74, 75, 80, 84, 87
    as super-ego, 73, 80

Reassurance, 76
Regression, 31

Reparation, 19, 28, 35, 49–50, 55, 57, 58, 67, 85, 87, 88
Repression, 73, 79, 85–6, 90
Riviere, J., 10n, 13, 93
Rosenfeld, H., 23n, 62n, 66, 94

Sanity
   envy of, 41, 72
   fear of loss of, 51–3
Saint Augustine, 40
Schizoid mechanisms (see also Splitting), 7n, 10, 13, 20, 23, 24, 33, 47ff., 52, 67, 68, 69, 73, 85, 87, 89, 91
Schizophrenia, 23n, 24, 30n, 62n, 67, 68, 85, 89
Sexuality (see Genital impulses)
Shakespeare, 8
Spenser, 40
Splitting
   and acting-out, 66
   analysing of, 12, 14, 43–60, 67, 72–4, 75–81, 85–90
   and fragmentation, 20, 23, 85, 89

of good and bad object, 4, 5, 13, 23–5, 62, 68, 82, 84
   and integration, 22–3, 24, 25–6, 28, 31, 43–60, 69, 70–81, 85–91
   of love and hate, 13, 14, 23, 24, 62ff., 69, 72ff., 85, 86ff.
   need for, 23–4, 62, 68, 82
   repression versus, 73, 79, 85–6, 89–90
Sublimation, 15, 19, 34, 42
Super-ego, 31, 40, 73, 85
Synthesis (see Ego)

Thinking
   disturbance in (see Confusion)
Transference (see also Psycho-analyst), 1–3, 11–14, 31, 63, 70ff., 86ff.

Urethral impulses, 68
Urethral sadism, 6n, 7, 47ff.

Winnicott, D. W., 19n, 94
Withdrawal, 63, 71